Better Homes and Gardens®

COUNTRY STENCILING

© Copyright 1988 by Meredith Corporation, Des Moines, Iowa.
All Rights Reserved. Printed in the United States of America.
First Edition. First Printing.
Library of Congress Catalog Card Number: 87-63203
ISBN: 0-696-01705-9 (hardcover)
ISBN: 0-696-01707-5 (trade paperback)

BETTER HOMES AND GARDENS® BOOKS

Editor: Gerald M. Knox
Art Director: Ernest Shelton
Managing Editor: David A. Kirchner
Editorial Project Managers: James D. Blume,
    Marsha Jahns, Rosanne Weber Mattson

Crafts Editor: Joan Cravens
Senior Crafts Editors: Beverly Rivers,
    Sara Jane Treinen
Associate Crafts Editor: Elizabeth Porter

Associate Art Directors: Neoma Thomas,
    Linda Ford Vermie, Randall Yontz
Assistant Art Directors: Lynda Haupert,
    Harijs Priekulis, Tom Wegner
Graphic Designers: Mary Schlueter Bendgen,
    Mike Burns, Brian Wignall
Art Production: Director, John Berg;
    Associate, Joe Heuer;
    Office Manager, Michaela Lester

President, Book Group: Jeramy Lanigan
Vice President, Retail Marketing: Jamie L. Martin
Vice President, Administrative Services: Rick Rundall

BETTER HOMES AND GARDENS® MAGAZINE
President, Magazine Group: James A. Autry
Vice President, Editorial Director: Doris Eby
Executive Director, Editorial Services: Duane L. Gregg

MEREDITH CORPORATION CORPORATE OFFICERS
Chairman of the Board: E. T. Meredith III
President: Robert A. Burnett
Executive Vice President: Jack D. Rehm

COUNTRY STENCILING
Editor: Sara Jane Treinen
Contributing Editor: Gary Boling
Editorial Project Manager: James D. Blume
Graphic Designer: Mary Schlueter Bendgen
Contributing Graphic Designer: Patricia Konecny
Electronic Text Processor: Paula Forest

Cover project: See page 57.

CONTENTS

HEARTS AND FLOWERS

FOR COUNTRY ROMANCE

The craft of stenciling has a beautifully rich past. Not only does its practice parallel our country's development, but examples of stenciling are found in centuries-old buildings all over the world. Today, a stenciling revival goes hand in hand with popular country looks. This chapter includes some romantic examples of this simple and ever-popular craft, including tabletop decorations, a stenciled picture mat, and several country accessories that make ideal first-time projects.

The motifs stenciled onto the wash bench, *opposite,* are reminiscent of Pennsylvania Dutch painted decorations. The main design consists of two hearts flanked by a symmetrical arrangement of flowers and leaves. A trailing vine of hearts and delicate leaves is used to trim the bench. These patterns are used—in various forms—to decorate a pair of wooden buckets, *opposite* and *left.*

Most of the stenciling on these projects is enhanced with shading and highlighting. These effects are easy to achieve with a stencil brush, and they add a three-dimensional look to your work. For more about shading and highlighting, see page 34.

Instructions and patterns for the projects shown in this chapter begin on page 12.

Painting heavy canvas with several coats of acrylic paint creates a surprisingly durable surface that is suitable for stenciling. Canvas treated in this way can be used for many home accessories, especially floorcloths (see pages 55 and 56–57) and other items that must withstand constant wear and tear.

Here, we've created a pair of place mats, *opposite,* and a matching table runner, *above.* The place mats are pieces of canvas cut into heart shapes; the table runner is a canvas strip with heart shapes (identical to the place mats') painted on the ends. You can adjust the length of the 18-inch-wide runner to best fit your table. Use the runner or the place mats on a small table, combine all three pieces on a large table, or make four place mats to fit around your entire table.

Many beginners find that stenciling with a few colors simplifies learning the technique, yet still yields striking projects. These table accessories, for example, use just purple and lavender (with touches of pink and white). The hearts are lavender stenciled with purple motifs; the remainder of the runner is purple stenciled with lavender motifs.

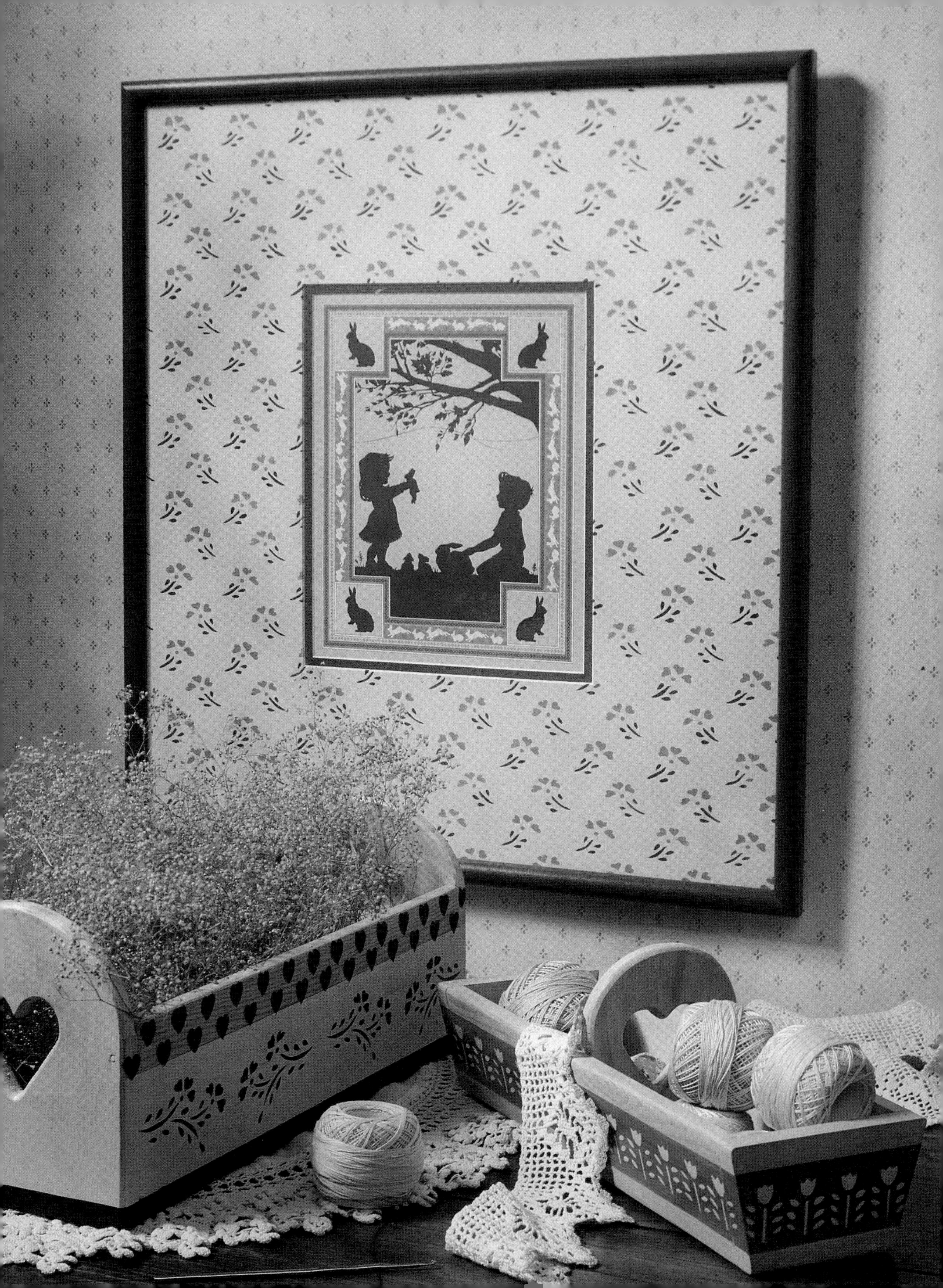

HEARTS AND FLOWERS

The projects on these two pages represent two distinct design approaches: smaller stencils repeated many times to cover an area and larger stencils combined for a single dramatic design. Either of these methods works quite well.

To assure that each of the stenciled motifs for the picture mat, *opposite,* lines up perfectly, lightly pencil a grid onto the mat board before beginning to stencil. Stencil all of the stems first with dark blue paint, aligning their positions with intersections on the grid. Then stencil flowers above each stem.

The fanciful flower designs on the two stenciled boxes, *opposite,* can be adapted to fit containers of various shapes and sizes. One box features a heart border stenciled over unpainted wood. The other box is pickled before it is painted, by applying diluted white paint, then wiping it away.

Notice that several of these projects share common design elements. The flower on the mat board is repeated on one of the boxes, and also appears as part of the vine on the shelf. Experiment with extracting some of the smaller motifs from the projects shown and using them on smaller items.

Simple wooden shelves like the one *above* are available where unfinished furniture is sold. Or, you can make a similar shelf from clear white pine—or strip the paint off a shelf salvaged from the attic. Begin stenciling the design with the center white flower, then add the mirror-image vines on each side.

HEARTS AND FLOWERS

Paint isn't the only material you can stencil with. For a change from conventional acrylic or latex paints, try working directly onto bare wood with wood stains or diluted stencil paints. Either technique enables the texture and pattern of the wood beneath to show through.

The designs on the jewelry box and the candle holder, *opposite,* are created with various shades of wood stain. This works best when the wood is left unfinished, but for stencil designs that require only one or two shades of stain, applying a coat of light stain to the background does not detract from the stenciled motifs.

The 14-inch-diameter plate, *above,* features a simple geometric design and just a few soft colors.

To add accents that are compatible with the bare wood surfaces, outline all or part of the design elements with a woodburning tool.

Wash Bench

Shown on page 4.

Finished bench is 11x20x32 inches.

MATERIALS
Basic stenciling and painting supplies
Base coat for bench: medium blue latex paint
Stencil paints: hunter green, dark blue, maroon, white, black, slate blue, and light blue
Paste wax; soft cloth
Polyurethane varnish
Clear white pine 1x12s: one 32-inch piece (top) ripped to 11 inches wide, and two 19¼-inch pieces (legs) ripped to 10½ inches wide
Clear white pine 1x6s: two 30-inch pieces (sides) ripped to 4¼ inches wide
Scraps of 1x1 and ¾x¾ wood for bracing
Wood screws; wood glue
Band saw or jigsaw

INSTRUCTIONS
Before beginning, see the Stenciling Primer, pages 74–79, for information on stenciling supplies, cutting stencils, and applying paint to stencil areas.
Cut a 4¾-inch-diameter half circle at bottom of each leg piece. Referring to the full-size pattern for the large heart-with-flowers motif, *opposite,* trace the large heart in the center and the small heart beneath it. Transfer this design to the legs, positioning the top of large heart 6⅜ inches below the tops of the leg pieces; cut out both heart shapes. Paint the legs with two coats of medium blue latex paint, sanding lightly between coats.

To make the stencils
Referring to the full-size pattern, *opposite,* cut stencils A, B, C, and D of large heart-with-flowers motif. Cut stencils A, B, and C of heart-border motif, *right.* Label

each stencil and transfer registration markings with a permanent marker.

To stencil the designs
BENCH TOP: Position and tape stencil A of heart-border motif so that bottom heart is 1 inch from one of the bench top's narrow ends. Stencil with maroon; shade the edges with dark blue and highlight with white. Repeat on other end. Then positon stencil A so that the bottom heart is 12 inches from one of the narrow ends of the bench top. Stencil as before; repeat on other end.
Position and tape stencil B on each stenciled border; stencil with hunter green.
Position and tape stencil C on each stenciled border. Stencil with hunter green; highlight tips with a mixture of hunter green and white; shade the inside of the tips lightly with black.

HEART-BORDER MOTIF STENCILS:

A
B
C

Fold

Position and tape stencil A of large heart-with-flowers motif so that bottom edges of lowest leaves are 4¼ inches from one of the narrow ends of the bench top. Stencil with hunter green; highlight with a mixture of hunter green and white from the tips inward about 1 inch. Highlight the flower stems ¼ to ⅜ inch up from their tips with white. Shade the leaves and flower stems with black.
Position and tape stencil B; stencil with slate blue. Shade edges of heart and lower edges of small petals with dark blue; highlight tops of petals with white. Highlight center area of heart with white; shade right side of heart with maroon.
Position and tape stencil C; stencil with maroon. Highlight small petals with white; shade with dark blue. Highlight upper flower petals with slate blue; shade with dark blue. Highlight heart with slate blue; shade with dark blue.
Position and tape stencil D; stencil with slate blue. Shade tips of petals with dark blue; shade bases of petals with maroon.
Repeat large heart-with-flowers motif on other side of bench top.

LEGS: Position and tape stencil A of heart border 2½ inches above tops of cutouts. Repeat steps as for outer borders of bench top.
Position and tape stencil A of large heart-with-flowers motif over the cutouts; blocking out the flower stems, stencil as for bench top. Position and tape stencil B; blocking out the small petals on each side, stencil as before. Position and tape stencil C; blocking out lower flower petals, stencil as before. Omit stencil D.

BENCH SIDES (optional): If desired, position and stencil three repeats of the heart-border motif along the sidepieces.
continued

LARGE HEART-WITH-FLOWERS MOTIF STENCILS:

A
B
C
D

To assemble the wash bench

Cut 1x1s into four 4-inch lengths and the ¾x¾-inch lumber into two 27½-inch lengths. Glue and screw a ¾x¾-inch piece along the top of one side of each sidepiece. Glue and screw the 1x1s below the ¾x¾ pieces, placing the 1x1s flush with the narrow ends.

Recessing sidepieces ¼ inch, glue and screw sidepieces to legs. Secure top to leg assembly.

With light blue paint, lightly trim all edges with small strokes; outline cutouts similarly. Highlight blue trim with white.

Seal with two coats of polyurethane varnish, sanding lightly between coats. Apply two coats of paste wax. Polish with a cloth.

Bucket with Lid

Shown on page 5.

MATERIALS

Basic stenciling and painting supplies
Bucket with lid: Bucket shown is item P1345 from Basketville, Inc.
Base coat for bucket: medium blue latex paint
Stencil paints: maroon, hunter green, camel, slate blue, black, walnut brown
Chalk pencil
Paste wax; soft cloth

INSTRUCTIONS

Before beginning, see the Stenciling Primer, pages 74–79, for information on stenciling supplies, cutting stencils, and applying paint to stencil areas.

Paint the bucket and lid inside and out with two coats of medium blue latex paint, sanding lightly between coats.

With a chalk pencil, mark centerline of lid; draw four vertical lines evenly spaced around the bucket.

To make the stencils

Referring to the full-size patterns, cut stencils A and C of the heart-border motif, page 12; cut stencils A, B, C, and D of the large heart-with-flowers motif, page 13. Label each stencil and transfer the registration markings with a permanent marker.

To stencil the designs

LID: Position and tape stencil B of the large heart-with-flowers motif. Stencil the heart with maroon; highlight with camel and shade with slate blue. Stencil the small petals with walnut brown; highlight with camel.

Position and tape stencil A. Stencil all parts with hunter green; highlight leaves and stems with camel; shade leaves and stems with black.

Position and tape stencil C. Stencil heart with walnut brown; highlight with camel; shade with maroon. Stencil small petals with maroon; highlight with camel. Stencil upper flower petals with slate blue; highlight with camel; shade with walnut brown and maroon.

Position and tape stencil D. Stencil lower petals camel; shade with walnut brown along tops of petals and with maroon along bottoms of petals.

BUCKET: Make overlays of heart-border design and of small heart and lowest pair of leaves from large heart-with-flowers motif. Plan position of four hearts evenly placed around bucket, each flanked by a pair of leaves. Plan border motif around bucket beneath hearts; invert pattern and repeat above hearts.

Position and tape stencil A of heart-border motif. Stencil with maroon; highlight with camel and shade with walnut brown. Position and tape stencil C; stencil with hunter green; highlight with camel and shade with walnut brown.

Stencil hearts from large motif with walnut brown; highlight with camel and shade with walnut brown.

Stencil leaves with hunter green; highlight with camel and shade with black.

Allow paint to dry. Seal with two coats of varnish, sanding lightly between coats. When dry, apply paste wax; polish.

SMALL HEART-WITH-FLOWERS MOTIF STENCILS:

A ▭
B ▨

Small Bucket

Shown on page 4.

MATERIALS
Basic stenciling and painting
  supplies
Wooden bucket: Bucket shown
  is item R1131 from
  Basketville, Inc.
Base coat for bucket: medium
  blue latex paint
Stencil paints: dark blue, white,
  slate blue, and black
Chalk pencil
Polyurethane varnish
Paste wax; soft cloth

INSTRUCTIONS
Before beginning, see the Stenciling Primer, pages 74–79, for information on stenciling supplies, cutting stencils, and applying paint to stencil areas.

Paint bucket inside and out with two coats of medium blue latex paint, sanding lightly between coats. With a chalk pencil, draw four vertical lines evenly spaced around bucket.

To make the stencils
Referring to the full-size patterns, cut stencils A, B, and C of the heart-border motif, page 12; cut stencils A and B of the small heart-with-flowers motif, *oppo-

FLOWER BORDER

site. Label each stencil and transfer registration markings with a permanent marker.

To stencil the designs
FRONT AND BACK: Position and tape stencil A of the heart-border motif so that the bottom of the heart is ⅜ inch above the lower band. Stencil with slate blue; shade with dark blue and highlight with white. Position and tape stencil B; stencil with dark blue. Position and tape stencil C; stencil with slate blue; shade with dark blue and highlight with white.

Position and tape stencil A of the small heart-with-flowers motif so that the bottom of the heart is 1⅜ inches above the lower band. Stencil the heart with white; shade with slate blue and dark blue. Stencil the small petals with slate blue; highlight with white and shade with dark blue.

Position and tape stencil B. Stencil with dark blue; highlight

the leaves first with slate blue and then with white.

SIDES: Position small heart-with-flowers motif on sides. Stencil as for front and back.

Seal with two coats of varnish, sanding lightly between coats. Apply paste wax and polish.

Wooden Box With Hearts

Shown on page 8.

MATERIALS
Basic stenciling and painting
  supplies
Pine box with heart cutouts in
  ends
Base coat for box: antique white
  latex paint
Stencil paints: barn red and
  medium green
Polyurethane varnish
continued

**BOX MOTIF
STENCILS:**

A
B

INSTRUCTIONS

Before beginning, see the Stenciling Primer, pages 74–79, for information on stenciling supplies, cutting stencils, and applying paint to stencil areas.

Make a tissue overlay of design, adjusting position of motifs to fit the sides of your box, if necessary.

With 1-inch-wide tape, mask stripes along the tops of the box sides. Paint box inside and out with antique white latex paint. When box is dry, mask off a ½-inch-wide stripe all around bottom; paint with barn red. When dry, remove all maskings. Mark centers of box sides.

To make the stencils

Referring to full-size pattern, page 15, cut stencils A and B of box motif. Label each stencil and transfer registration markings with a permanent marker.

To stencil the designs

Tape stencil A to left portion of one side of box, placing the top hearts within the unfinished stripe at the top of the box; stencil with barn red. Let stencil dry; reverse, tape to right portion of box side, and stencil with barn red.

Position stencil B; stencil with medium green. Repeat stencils A and B on other side of box.

Seal with two coats of polyurethane varnish, sanding lightly between coats.

Wooden Box With Flowers

Shown on page 8.

MATERIALS

Basic stenciling and painting supplies
Unfinished pine box with center handle: Box shown is 2½x4½x11½ inches.
Base coat for box: antique white latex paint
Stencil paints: antique white and medium blue
Clean rags
Polyurethane varnish

INSTRUCTIONS

Before beginning, see the Stenciling Primer, pages 74–79, for information on stenciling supplies, cutting stencils, and applying paint to stencil areas.

Dilute antique white latex paint with water to a milky consistency. Wipe onto box with a clean rag; remove excess with a second rag. Set thinned paint aside for later use. With tape, mask off a 1½-inch-wide stripe, centered, around sides of box; paint stripe medium blue. When dry, remove masking and mark centers of box sides and ends.

To make the stencils

Referring to the full-size pattern, page 15, cut stencil for flow-er border. Transfer registration markings with a permanent marker.

To stencil the designs

Beginning at centers of sides and ends, position and tape flower border; stencil with antique white stencil paint.

When stenciling is completed and paint is dry, *lightly* wipe thinned antique white latex paint over stenciling. Seal with two coats of polyurethane varnish, sanding lightly between coats.

Shelf

Shown on page 9.

MATERIALS

Basic stenciling and painting supplies
Unfinished pine shelf with top rail sufficiently large for stenciled design that is 6½x25 inches
Base coat for shelf: light blue latex paint
Stencil paints: white, dark blue, barn red, medium green, and yellow
Clean rags
Polyurethane varnish

continued

B

Match Line AB

A

Fold

**SHELF MOTIF
STENCILS:**

A
B
C
D

A —————————————— **Match Line AB** —————————————— B

HEARTS AND FLOWERS

INSTRUCTIONS

Before beginning, see the Stenciling Primer, pages 74–79, for information on stenciling supplies, cutting stencils, and applying paint to stencil areas.

Dilute the light blue latex paint to a milky consistency. Wipe the paint onto the pine with a clean rag; wipe off excess with a second rag. The grain of the wood will show through.

To make the stencils

Referring to the full-size patterns, pages 16–17, trace the complete pattern by aligning the two portions of the pattern at line AB. Reverse pattern and complete flowering vine toward the right of big flower (see photo, page 9). Cut stencils A, B, C, and D of this shelf motif. Note that slightly half of stencil B and all of stencils C and D are to be reversed to complete the design. Label each stencil and transfer registration markings with a permanent marker.

To stencil the designs

Position and tape stencil A; stencil with white.

Position and tape stencil B with short vines between white petals and long vine trailing to one side; stencil with medium green. When dry, reverse stencil and stencil remaining vine on other side.

Position and tape stencil C on one side; stencil with barn red. Reverse stencil and stencil other side.

Position and tape stencil D on one side; stencil with dark blue. Reverse and stencil other side.

With yellow, paint small dots freehand in centers of 13 barn red flowers, as well as one larger dot in center of large white flower.

Sand away the paint on portions of the shelf edges. Seal with two coats of polyurethane varnish, sanding lightly between coats.

Mat Board

Shown on page 8.

MATERIALS

Basic stenciling supplies
Cream mat board: Stencil a piece slightly larger than picture frame
Stencil paints: medium blue and dark blue
Mat cutter
Cork-backed metal ruler
Soft pencil; kneaded eraser

INSTRUCTIONS

Before beginning, see the Stenciling Primer, pages 74–79, for information on stenciling supplies, cutting stencils, and applying paint to stencil areas.

Using ruler and soft pencil, *lightly* mark a 1-inch grid over entire surface of mat board.

To make the stencils

Referring to full-size pattern, *below*, cut stencils A and B. Label each stencil and transfer registration markings with a permanent marker.

To stencil the designs

Referring to the pattern, align stencil A on grid so that centers of motifs align with alternate intersections of grid. Tape in place and stencil with dark blue. Repeat until surface of mat board is covered.

Position and tape stencil B; stencil with medium blue.

When all paint is *thoroughly* dry, erase grid marks with kneaded eraser.

Mark position of cutout with pencil, centering within flower motifs. Following manufacturer's directions, use mat cutter and cork-backed ruler to cut out center opening. Trim mat to correct size and secure in frame.

Wooden Box

Shown on page 10.

MATERIALS

Basic stenciling supplies
Unfinished wooden box with hinged lid: Box shown is 3¾x4¾x8⅞ inches.
Gel wood stain: 4 different shades, ranging from dark to light
3/16-inch-wide rule tape (available at commercial-art-supply stores)
Small sharp knife
Woodburning tool
Polyurethane varnish

INSTRUCTIONS

Before beginning, see the Stenciling Primer, pages 74–79, for information on stenciling supplies, cutting stencils, and applying paint to stencil areas.

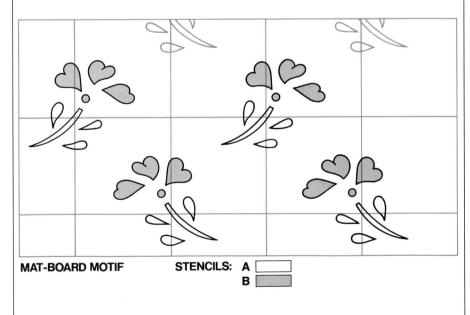

MAT-BOARD MOTIF   STENCILS: A [ ]
B [▨]

To make the stencils

Referring to the full-size pattern, *below*, cut stencils A and B. Cut stencil C, extending it the full width of the box top. Label each stencil and transfer registration markings with a permanent marking pen.

To stencil the designs

Position and tape stencil A to box top; stencil with lightest shade of stain, applying stain slightly more heavily toward center of flower. (See tip on page 34 for more information on shading stenciled areas.)

Position and tape stencil B; stencil with next darkest shade of stain.

Position and tape stencil C above and below flower and leaves. With masking tape, mask stripes down front and back of box to align with stripe on top; stencil with the next to the darkest shade of stain.

When first three shades of stain are dry, etch outlines of leaves and flower petals with woodburning tool. Add veins to leaves, accents to flower petals, and dots to flower center.

For the dark stripes, mask areas already stenciled. To mask the leaves that will abut the dark stripes, cover leaves and surrounding areas with masking tape; using a small sharp knife, cut along woodburned edge to and remove excess tape.

Using artist's rule tape, mask off five small stripes parallel to large stained stripe. Extend the small stripes partially down the front of the box. Place a wide strip of masking tape at an angle at the ends of the stripes to form tapered ends (see photo, page 10). Stencil stripes with the darkest shade of stain.

Seal with two coats of polyurethane varnish, sanding lightly between coats. (*Note:* Carefully sand woodburned edges; too much sanding will lighten the lines.)

Table Runner and Place Mats

Shown on pages 6–7.

MATERIALS:
Basic stenciling and painting supplies
Heavy artist's canvas: 20x46-inch piece for runner and 15x19-inch piece for each place mat
Purple and white latex paints
Pink stencil paint; chalk pencil
Water-base primer
Plywood; staple gun; staples
Polyurethane varnish

INSTRUCTIONS

Before beginning, see the Stenciling Primer, pages 74–79, for information on stenciling supplies, cutting stencils, and applying paint to stencil areas.

See Flower-Patterned Floorcloth instructions, pages 65–66, *continued*

WOODEN-BOX MOTIF STENCILS:

A
B
C

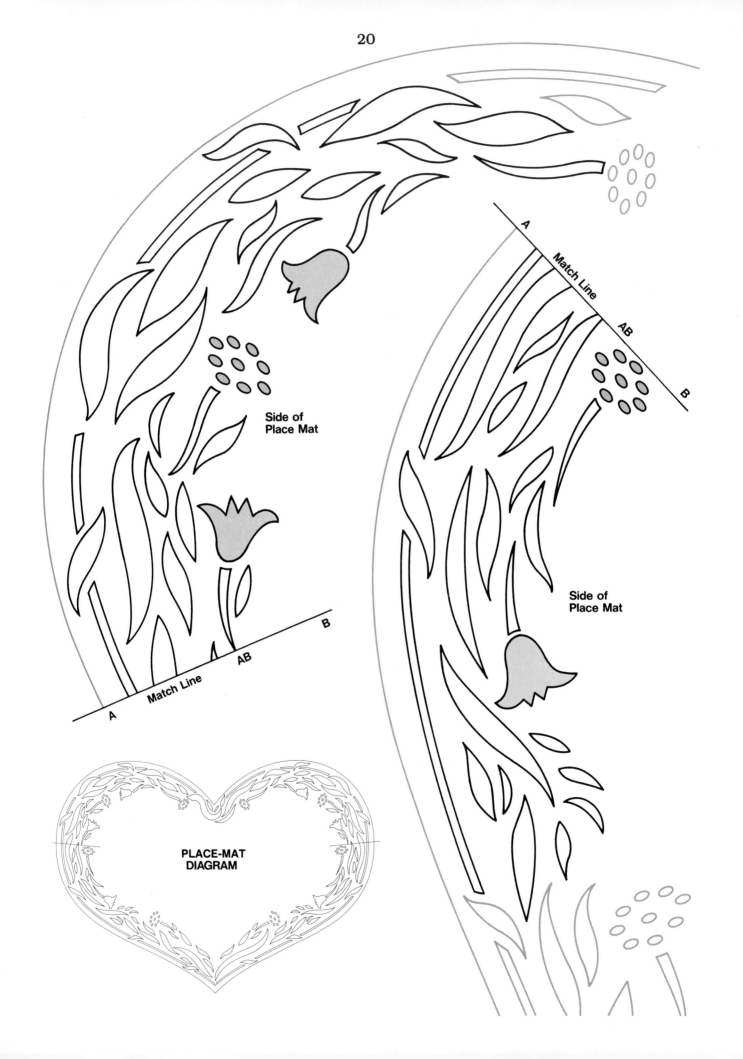

A

Match Line

AB

B

Side of
Place Mat

B

AB

Match Line

A

Side of
Place Mat

**PLACE-MAT
DIAGRAM**

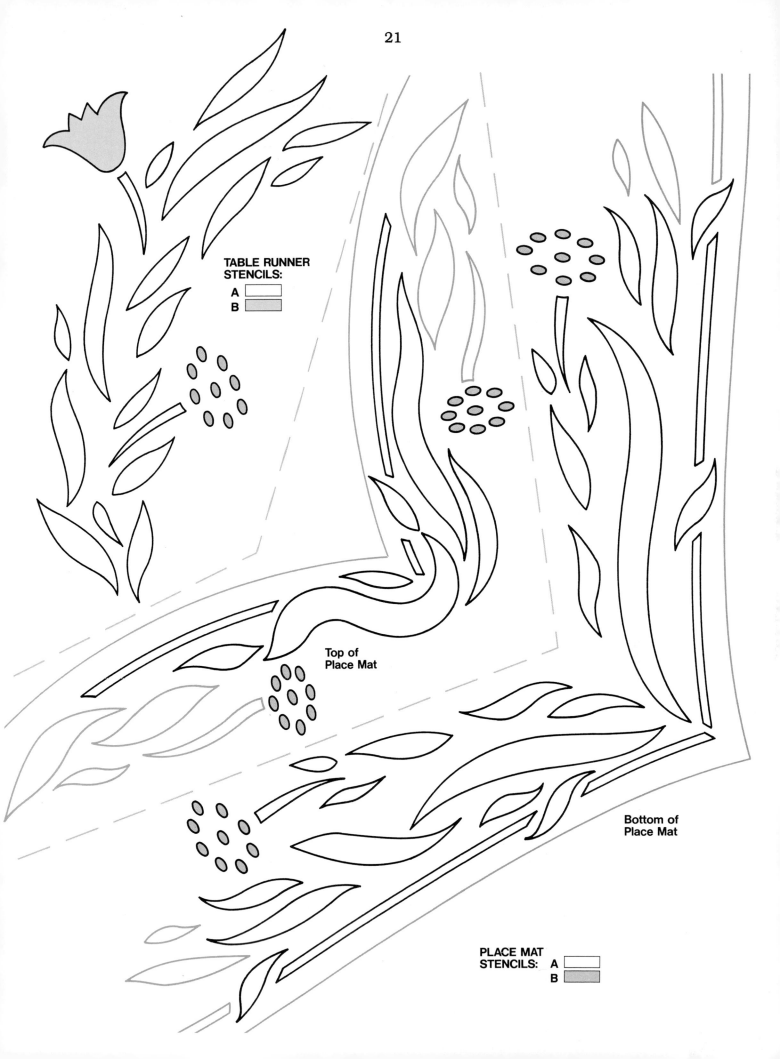

TABLE RUNNER
STENCILS:

A
B

Top of
Place Mat

Bottom of
Place Mat

PLACE MAT
STENCILS: A
B

CANDLE-HOLDER MOTIF STENCILS:

A
B
C
D

to stretch and prime canvas. Referring to full-size patterns, pages 20–21, trace and connect the four portions of the large heart shape. Outline outer edges with a marker. Transfer heart shape to canvas. Cut one shape from canvas for each place mat. For runner, cut canvas to an 18x44-inch piece. Transfer heart pattern to each end of strip; cut away excess.

Mix purple and white latex paints to make lavender; paint each place mat lavender. Paint heart shapes on ends of runner lavender; paint remaining area of runner purple.

To make the stencils

Referring to the full-size patterns, pages 20–21, cut stencils A and B of place-mat motif. Cut stencils A and B of table-runner motif. Label each stencil and transfer registration markings with a permanent marker.

To stencil the designs

Position and tape stencil A of place-mat motif to place mat; stencil with purple. Position and tape stencil B; stencil with pink. Repeat both stencils on ends of runner (lavender areas). Paint nine white dots freehand on ends of remaining stems.

Position and tape stencil A of table-runner motif to purple area of runner; stencil with lavender. Position and tape stencil B; stencil with pink. Paint white dots freehand as before.

Seal runner and mats with one or two coats of polyurethane varnish, sanding lightly between coats.

Candle Holder

Shown on page 10.

MATERIALS
Basic stenciling and painting
   supplies
Unfinished, unassembled
   candle-holder kit
Gel wood stain in light, medium,
   and dark shades
Black stencil paint
Polyurethane varnish

Fold

HEARTS AND FLOWERS

Fold

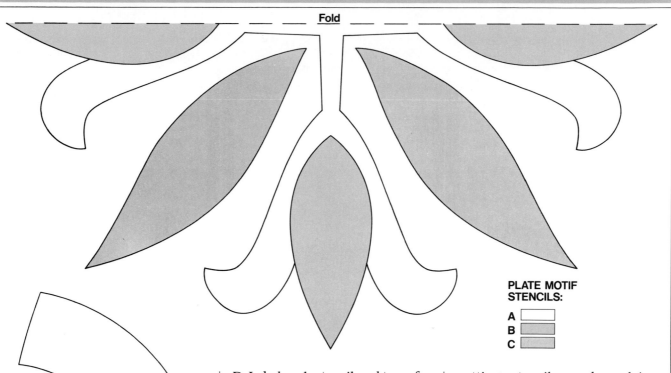

PLATE MOTIF STENCILS:

A
B
C

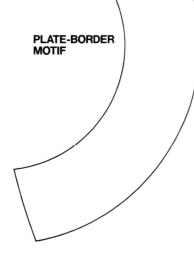

PLATE-BORDER MOTIF

INSTRUCTIONS

Before beginning, see the Stenciling Primer, pages 74–79, for information on stenciling supplies, cutting stencils, and applying paint to stencil areas.

To make the stencils

Referring to full-size pattern, *opposite,* complete candle-holder motif and cut stencils A, B, C, and D. Label each stencil and transfer registration markings with a permanent marker.

To stencil the designs

Position and tape stencil A near bottom of back of candle holder; stencil with black paint. Position stencil B; stencil with lightest shade of stain. Position stencil C; stencil with medium shade of stain. Position stencil D; stencil with darkest shade of stain.

Assemble candle holder. Seal with two coats of polyurethane varnish, sanding lightly between coats.

Plate

Shown on page 11.

MATERIALS
Basic stenciling supplies
14-inch-diameter unfinished wooden plate
Stencil paints: medium green, deep rose, pink, and light pink
Chalk pencil; light oak stain
Polyurethane varnish

INSTRUCTIONS

Before beginning, see the Stenciling Primer, pages 74–79, for information on stenciling supplies, cutting stencils, and applying paint to stencil areas.

Mark horizontal and vertical centerlines on plate with a chalk pencil; then mark 45-degree diagonal lines.

To make the stencils

Referring to full-size pattern, *above,* complete plate motif and cut stencils A, B, and C. Cut stencil for plate-border motif, *left.* Label each stencil and transfer registration markings with a permanent marker.

To stencil the designs

Thin paints slightly with water to make washes; use very small amounts of paint on brushes while stenciling. Position and tape stencil A; stencil with medium green. Position and tape stencil B; stencil with deep rose. Position and tape stencil C; stencil with light pink.

Center and tape border motif on one of the chalk lines; stencil with pink. Repeat around plate.

Paint a 1-inch-wide stripe around rim with light pink. With medium green, paint a ½-inch-wide stripe around rim of plate atop the light pink.

Cover plate with a light application of stain; let dry. Seal with two coats of polyurethane varnish, sanding lightly between coats.

HANDY TOTES

FOR WORK AND PLAY

It's easy to transform ordinary baskets and boxes into stylish accessories with just a stenciled motif or two. We designed the stencil motifs in this chapter to fit onto easy-to-locate unpainted objects, including splint baskets with attached lids, a wooden box, and an unfinished lap desk. If the designs shown don't fit your container, try reducing or enlarging the patterns, or experiment with border designs.

The focal points of the charming picnic accessories, *left* and *opposite,* are stenciled baskets filled with luscious apples. Use only three stencils to duplicate this handsome design—one for the basket, one for the apples, and one for the leaves.

A pair of additional stencils can be used to create the borders shown here. A row of evenly spaced cutouts forms a checkerboard edging on the lid of the picnic basket; see the tip on page 34 for more information on stenciling checks. A line of irregular checks, interrupted by small apples, is just right along the edge of the pie carrier.

Let the size and shape of your picnic basket determine how you use the stencils. First make note of your lid's dimensions. Then, using the dimensions and shapes of the patterns on pages 30–31 as a guide, plan the placement of the basket and border designs.

Instructions and patterns for the projects in this chapter begin on page 30.

The pleasing silhouette of a pair of tulips makes a perfect stencil motif. Our version is used to decorate a lap desk, *above* and *opposite,* inside and out.

Because the large tulip motif on the outside of the lid is reversed to make the design on the inside of the lid, stencil-cutting is kept to a minimum. In addition, the same bow motif is repeated for all of the bouquets as well as the ribbon trim along the top edge.

A still-smaller version of this design is just the right size to decorate the stationery, *above* and *opposite.* All of the stenciling shown here uses the shading and highlighting methods described on page 34.

Sewing and mending chores go easier when your equipment and supplies are nearby.

The stenciled button box, *above,* is a good project for beginners. Just cut one button stencil and repeat it randomly across the box top. Paint the holes in the buttons freehand.

The sewing basket, *opposite,* is embellished with some of the tools of the seamstress' trade. These simple shapes are easy to cut and stencil. You can cut a stencil of the curving length of thread, or, if you're comfortable with a paintbrush, you can add the thread with quick strokes.

If you select black as the base-coat color, you might have to stencil these designs first in white and then stencil them again in the colors shown here.

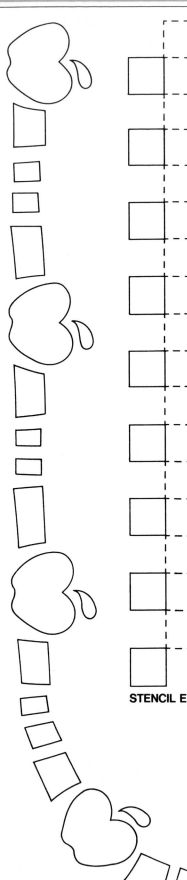

STENCIL E

STENCIL D

Picnic Basket

Shown on page 24.

Apple-basket motif is 6¼x6¾ inches.

MATERIALS
Basic stenciling and painting
  supplies
Rectangular picnic basket with
  10x21-inch hinged lid: Basket
  shown is item K206 from
  Basketville, Inc.
Base coat for basket: medium
  blue dye or medium blue
  spray paint
Stencil paints: maroon, camel,
  brown, hunter green, white,
  dark blue
Antiquing liquid; soft cloth
Polyurethane varnish

INSTRUCTIONS
Before beginning, see the Stenciling Primer, pages 74–79, for information on stenciling supplies, cutting stencils, and applying paint to stencil areas.

Paint or dye the picnic basket blue inside and out. Let the basket dry. Using a small paintbrush, apply antiquing liquid to the basket; do only small areas at a time; remove excess with a soft cloth. (Practice this technique on the bottom, if necessary.) Allow the basket to dry.

To make the stencils
Referring to full-size patterns, cut stencils A, B, and C of applebasket motif, *opposite;* cut one apple and one leaf motif from stencil D, *left;* and cut stencil E, *left.* Label each stencil and transfer registration markings with a permanent marker.

To stencil the designs
Mask the rounded corners of the basket lid with masking tape ¼ inch from the edges; don't mask the straight edges. Position and tape stencil E. Stencil ¼ inch away from the edges all around with maroon and a ½-inch brush. Stencil directly over the tape in the corners. Connect the checks logically, easing them around corners to fit.

Position and tape stencil A about 2 inches up from one end of the basket. Stencil with camel and a ½-inch brush; shade with brown and a ¼-inch brush.

Position and tape stencil B. Stencil with maroon and a ½-inch brush; shade with dark blue and a ¼-inch brush; highlight with white and a ⅛-inch brush.

Position and tape stencil C. Stencil with hunter green and a ½-inch brush; highlight with white and a ⅛-inch brush.

Repeat these three stencils on the other side of the lid.

Randomly stencil apples and leaves from stencil D on the slats of the basket.

Let basket dry; apply two coats of varnish, sanding lightly between coats.

Pie Carrier

Shown on page 25.

Apple-basket motif is 6¼x6¾ inches.

MATERIALS
Basic stenciling and painting
  supplies
Square picnic basket with
  13¼x13¼-inch hinged lid:
  Basket shown is item K84
  from Basketville, Inc.
Base coat for basket: light peach
  latex paint
Stencil paints: maroon, camel,
  brown, hunter green, white
Chalk pencil
Polyurethane varnish

INSTRUCTIONS
Before beginning, see the Stenciling Primer, pages 74–79, for information on stenciling supplies,

cutting stencils, and applying paint to stencil areas.

Sand rough spots off basket slats before painting. Paint the basket with two coats of the base coat inside and out, sanding the top lightly between coats. Let the basket dry. With a chalk pencil, mark centerlines of basket lid.

To make the stencils

Referring to the full-size patterns, cut stencils A, B, and C of the apple-basket motif, *below;* cut stencil D, *opposite,* for border. Label stencils and transfer any registration markings with a permanent marker.

To stencil the designs

Referring to the instructions for the Picnic Basket, *opposite,* stencil the apple-basket motif at the center of the lid, omitting the dark blue shading on stencil B.

For the border around the lid, use stencil D. Stencil an apple in each corner first with maroon and a ½-inch brush; highlight with white and a ⅛-inch brush. Stencil the leaves with hunter green. Add apples and leaves evenly spaced to edges of lid. Using rectangles from stencil D, fill in spaces between apples with brown and a ¼-inch brush.

Let basket dry; apply two coats of varnish, sanding lightly between coats.

Lap Desk

Shown on pages 26–27.

Large tulip motif is 7½x9 inches.

MATERIALS

Basic stenciling and painting supplies
Lap desk: Lid of desk shown is 10½x16⅜ inches.
Base coat for lap desk: pale pink latex paint
Stencil paints: pink, plum, light loden green, berry red, hunter green, white, slate blue, dark blue
Chalk pencil
Polyurethane varnish

continued

APPLE-BASKET MOTIF STENCILS:

A
B
C

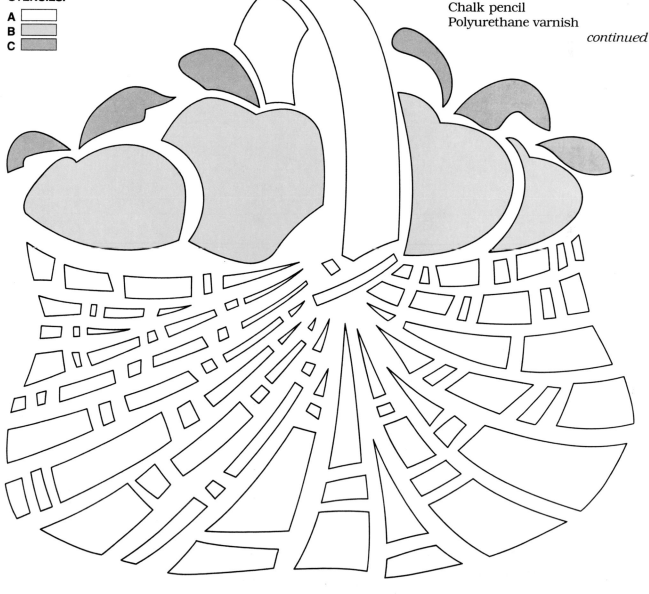

HANDY TOTES FOR WORK AND PLAY

RIBBON MOTIF

LARGE TULIP MOTIF
STENCILS:

A
B
C
D

INSTRUCTIONS

Before beginning, see the Stenciling Primer, pages 74–79, for information on stenciling supplies, cutting stencils, and applying paint to stencil areas.

Remove the hinges from the lid; sand lid. Paint all surfaces of desk and lid with base coat. Let dry.

To make the stencils

Referring to full-size patterns, cut stencils for large tulip motif (stencils A–D), *opposite;* small tulip motif (stencils A and B), *below;* and ribbon motif, *opposite.* (Note that stencils C and D from the large motif are repeated on the small tulip motif; these stencils are also used again for the ribbon trim.) Label each stencil and transfer registration markings with a marker.

To position tulips, trace each tulip motif; lay tissue patterns on desk lid.

(*Note:* This project requires reversing certain stencils; let each stencil dry thoroughly before turning it over.)

To stencil the designs

OUTSIDE OF LID: Referring to photograph on page 27, position and tape stencil A of large tulip motif to left side of lid. Stencil with pink and ½-inch brush. With ¼-inch brushes, shade with berry red near centers of large petals and near tops of background petals; shade with plum near bottoms of petals. With ⅛-inch brush, highlight with white.

Position and tape stencil B. Stencil with light loden green and ½-inch brush; shade with hunter green and a ½-inch brush; highlight with white and a ⅛-inch brush.

Position and tape stencil C. Stencil with slate blue and a ½-inch brush; shade with dark blue and a ¼-inch brush.

Position and tape stencil D. Stencil as for stencil C.

Position and tape stencil A of small tulip motif to right side of lid; stencil as for stencil A of large tulip motif.

Position and tape stencil B; stencil as for stencil B of large tulip motif.

Position and repeat stencils C and D from large tulip motif onto small tulip motif.

Set lid aside.

TOP TRIM: Position and tape stencils C and D along top edge of lap desk; stencil and shade as before.

Position stencil for ribbon motif adjacent to stenciled bow; stencil as for stencil C. Let ribbon-motif stencil dry thoroughly; reverse the stencil and stencil on opposite side of stenciled bow.

INSIDE OF LID: After top of lid is *thoroughly dry,* place underside faceup on a clean work surface. Position the large tulip motif on the side opposite to the large tulip motif on the lid top. Repeat stencils A, B, C, and D as for top of lid.

Let lid dry; apply two coats of varnish, sanding lightly between coats. Reattach the hinges.

Stationery

Shown on pages 26–27.

MATERIALS

Basic stenciling and painting supplies
Plain stationery
Stencil paints: pink, berry red, hunter green, dark blue

continued

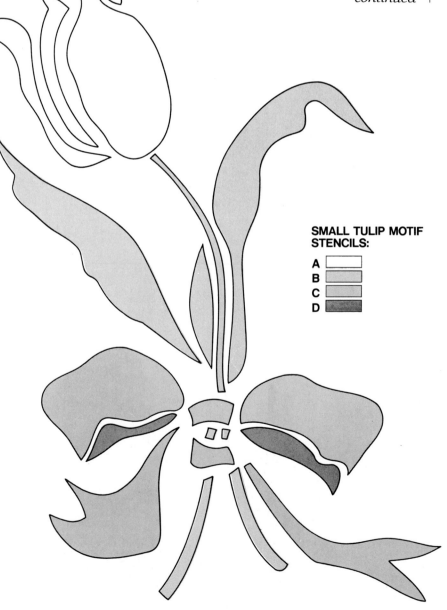

SMALL TULIP MOTIF
STENCILS:

A
B
C
D

HANDY TOTES FOR WORK AND PLAY

Shading and Highlighting Stenciled Areas

Several of the projects in this book are specially stenciled to create three-dimensional effects. This treatment, which uses shading and highlighting, offers a contrast to flat painted areas.

One-color effects

To create a three-dimensional look with just one color of stencil paint, vary the coverage of paint to darken and lighten areas. How you do this depends upon the relative darkness and lightness of the base coat and the stencil paint. If the base coat is lighter than the stencil paint, apply more paint to shade an area and less paint to highlight it. If the base coat is darker than the stencil paint, stencil lightly in shaded areas and more heavily in highlighted areas.

For stenciled areas where the base coat is lighter than the stencil paint, for example, use the following two methods for one-color shading.

First, try varying the amount of paint applied to a shape. For example, to stencil a circle so that it appears to be a sphere, stencil a very dark application of paint in the lower portion of the circle. Continue filling in the circle, applying less paint as you work toward the top.

An alternate method is to cover a stenciled area very lightly; let the paint dry and repeat, covering less of the stenciled area with successive applications.

Multicolor effects

Using two or more colors to shade and highlight requires a bit more brush control and some knowledge of how color values interact. The technique is quite easy to master, however, and the appearance of a stenciled area with multicolor shading and highlighting can be striking.

First, stencil an entire area with a middle value and let the paint dry. Leave the stencil in place and, using a lighter color or a lighter shade of the same color, stencil just a portion of the area and let it dry. Then, using a darker color or a darker shade of the same color, stencil the opposite side of the stenciled area. Blend the colors as you work, feathering the second and third applications of paint into the first coat. Use the one-color shading techniques described above to blend colors smoothly.

Points to remember

When shading and highlighting, as with other painting techniques, imagine a light source on the images you're creating. For example, if you're stenciling several fruit shapes, keep in mind that the highlights on one round shape should be similarly positioned on another round shape. It doesn't matter whether the light areas are at center top or slightly to the left or the right of the center. Strive to keep the highlights and shadows consistently placed from shape to shape.

Pay attention, too, to the contrast between the stenciled shapes and the background color. In some instances, lack of contrast is desirable. Dark areas stenciled onto a dark background can take on a rich, warm appearance, and light shapes stenciled onto a light background can appear delicate and airy.

Stenciling Checks and Stripes

Accents such as checks and stripes are some of the trademarks of country decoration. Fortunately, they're easy to stencil onto painted surfaces.

Creating checkerboards

Covering an area with checks requires a bit of planning and some arithmetic.

Begin by cutting the stencil for the checks. True checkerboard patterns are made up of squares that touch at every corner; cutting a stencil to do this is impossible because the necessary cuts leave you with a pile of acetate squares. It's easier to cut a single row of checks, separating the cutout squares with uncut squares of equal size. (For 1-inch checks, cut a series of 1-inch squares spaced 1 inch apart.) Stencil one row of checks, then move the same stencil to the next row, offsetting its placement to form a checkerboard.

For rows of checks that are longer than your stencil, draw a baseline with a chalk pencil before beginning. Align all checks in the first row on this line.

Making stripes

Although stripes are among the easiest accents to stencil, there are a few methods to perfect your efforts.

Most stripes are made by either affixing two straight pieces of tape to a surface and stenciling the area between them, or by affixing one piece of tape to the painted background and painting the background again with another color.

To assure crisp edges along the stripe, make sure that the tape tightly adheres to the surface. Press along the tape's length, but don't press so tightly that the background color will pull away when the tape is removed.

To make sure that your stripes aren't wavy, draw a guideline onto the painted surface before affixing the tape. Some masking tapes are not stable and, when pulled from a roll, will pucker along the edges. For perfect stripes, use better-quality tapes, such as those used by commercial artists.

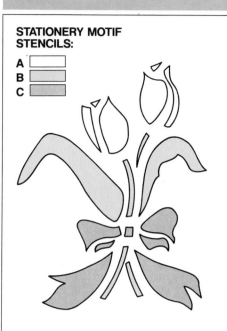

**STATIONERY MOTIF
STENCILS:**

A
B
C

INSTRUCTIONS

Before beginning, see the Stenciling Primer, pages 74–79, for information on stenciling supplies, cutting stencils, and applying paint to stencil areas.

To make the stencils

Referring to full-size pattern, *above,* cut stencils A, B, and C of stationery tulip motif. Label each stencil and transfer registration markings.

To stencil the designs

Position stencil A as desired on sheet of stationery. Stencil with a mixture of pink and berry red; shade lower portions of the petals with berry red.

Position stencil B; stencil with hunter green.

Position stencil C; stencil with dark blue.

Sewing Basket

Shown on page 29.

MATERIALS

Basic stenciling and painting supplies
Rectangular sewing basket with hinged lid: Lid on basket shown is 13x13 inches
Base coat for basket: flat black latex paint
Stencil paints: medium gray, black, light golden yellow, medium green, pink, red, bright yellow, and violet
Polyurethane varnish

INSTRUCTIONS

Before beginning, see the Stenciling Primer, pages 74–79, for information on stenciling supplies, cutting stencils, and applying paint to stencil areas.

Remove hinges from lid sections and handles. Paint all pieces of the basket with flat black latex paint; paint notions tray flat black and set aside.

To make the stencils

Referring to full-size patterns, pages 36–37, cut stencil A (scissors), B (needle), C (spool), and D (thread). Cut a stencil of a ¼-inch-diameter circle for scissors screw. Label the stencils and transfer registration markings with a permanent marker.

Before beginning, make a tissue overlay of completed design. Referring to photograph on page 29, adjust placement of motifs to fit your basket's shape. You can fill some areas with the button stencil used to decorate the button box shown on page 28; see instructions, *right.*

Draw a length of thread onto tissue overlay, beginning at spool closest to scissors point, taking it through needle's eye, then curling beneath needle. Cut a ⅛-inch-wide stencil of this shape. (You may opt to paint the length of thread freehand; lightly draw the thread in place with chalk pencil; paint with a small paintbrush.)

To stencil the designs

(*Note:* If your basket lid is split, slide the pieces together and tape them to the work surface.) Position and tape stencil A; stencil with medium gray. When scissors shape is dry, position and tape ¼-inch-diameter-circle stencil; stencil with black.

Position and tape stencil B; stencil with medium gray.

Position and tape stencil C; stencil with light golden yellow. Repeat four times.

Let all stenciled areas dry.

Position and tape stencil D between stencil C. Stencil with medium green, pink, red, bright yellow, and violet.

Position and tape thread stencil; stencil with color to match beginning spool of thread.

Let basket dry; apply two coats of varnish, sanding lightly between coats.

Reattach hinges.

Button Box

Shown on page 28.

MATERIALS

Basic stenciling and painting supplies
Small wooden box with hinged lid
Base coats for box: medium pink latex paint and medium rose latex paint
Stencil paints: medium rose, medium green, bright yellow, violet, medium blue, and black
Polyurethane varnish

INSTRUCTIONS

Before beginning, see the Stenciling Primer, pages 74–79, for information on stenciling supplies, cutting stencils, and applying paint to stencil areas.

Remove hinges from box. Paint box lid with medium pink latex paint and bottom of box with medium rose latex paint.

To make the stencils

Cut a ½-inch-diameter circle from a scrap of stencil material.

To stencil the designs

With a pencil, mark centers and colors of about 20 buttons randomly spaced on box top. If box sides are sufficiently tall, mark positions along sides of box, if desired.

Position and tape button stencil at center of each mark; stencil.

With small paintbrush, make two small black dots in center of each button.

Let box pieces dry; varnish with two coats, sanding lightly between coats. Reattach hinges.

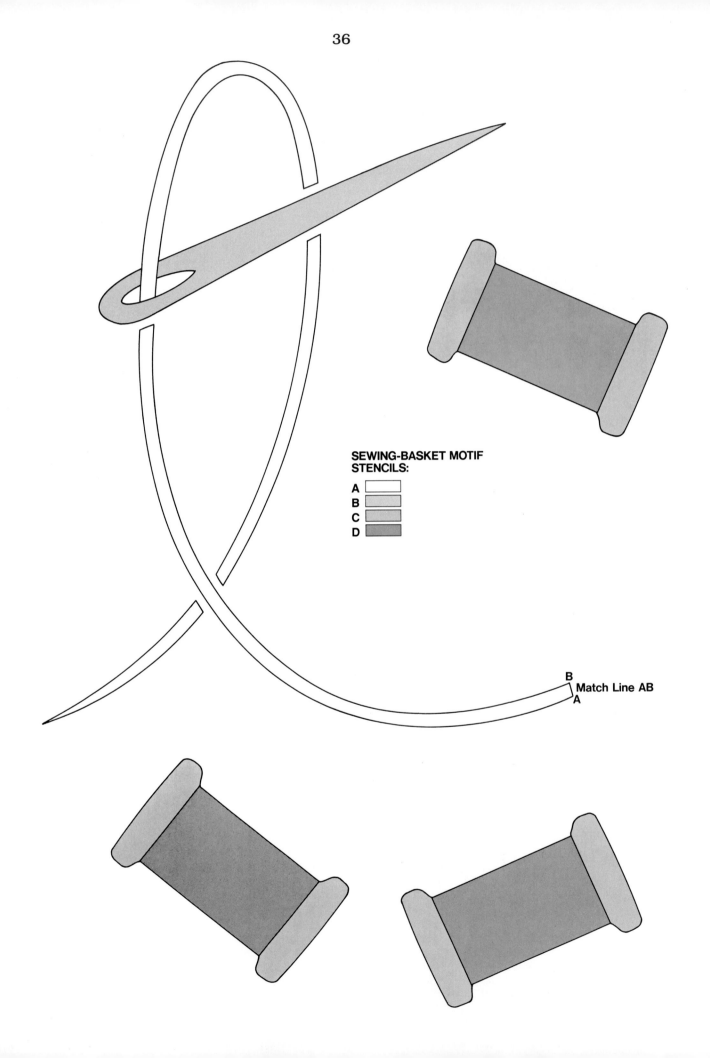

SEWING-BASKET MOTIF STENCILS:

A
B
C
D

B
Match Line AB
A

HANDY TOTES FOR WORK AND PLAY

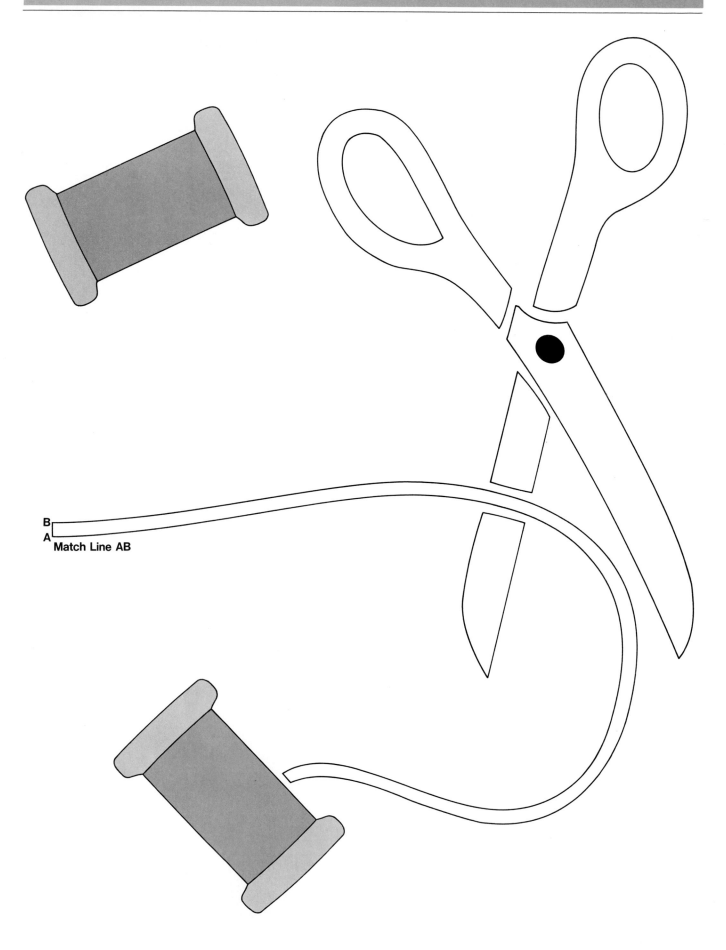

B
A
Match Line AB

A BUNNY FAMILY

FOR BABY'S ROOM

What a delightful room for a new baby!
The mother-bunny and father-bunny
motifs used for the projects in this
chapter appear in four sizes, ranging
from 4½-inch-high figures on a peg
rack to 12-inch-high stuffed toys.
Baby bunny, in a beribboned basket,
and heart motifs in two sizes
accompany the bunnies.

The nursery projects in
this chapter illustrate
how easy it is to use
stenciling to decorate a
room. These motifs
work equally well when
stenciled onto painted
surfaces or onto fabric.

A stenciled ruffle is a
beautiful way to trim
the bassinet, *opposite*.
The steps for stenciling
onto fabric are identical
to those for stenciling
onto painted surfaces.
For best results,

however, wash, dry, and
press the fabric before
stenciling onto it.

To decorate a piece of
furniture, such as the
rocking chair, *right*,
make sure that there
are sufficient flat areas
to stencil. Both sizes of
the heart-with-leaves
motifs from this chapter
fit onto this chair.

Instructions and
patterns for the projects
in this chapter begin on
page 44.

A BUNNY FAMILY FOR BABY'S ROOM

To make the cutout figures, *above* and *opposite,* and all of the smaller cutouts in this chapter, first trace the stencil patterns for the bunnies' outlines. Then transfer the outlines onto wood and cut the shapes with a jigsaw or band saw. Paint the cutouts and stencil the clothing and other features in place. Draw the faces with a permanent brown marker.

Stenciled versions of the large-bunny figures are used on the front of the toy box, *opposite.* This surface is big enough to include the baby bunny and a picket-fence border, as well as a heart-with-leaves motif on the top rail.

There are plenty of other imaginative uses for these bunny motifs. Repeat the bunnies and fence patterns to stencil a border onto the wall. Or make a headboard for your child's first bed from plywood, then stencil the toy-box design onto it.

A BUNNY FAMILY FOR BABY'S ROOM

Incorporate stenciling with woodworking and embroidery to create these bunny projects.

The peg rack, *opposite,* uses scraps of lumber and purchased pegs. These bunny figures are the smallest in the chapter, and are backed by a wooden heart cutout and a picket fence.

Use a pair of the medium-size bunnies for the lamp base, *opposite.* You can make and wire the lamp yourself with easy-to-find fittings and parts. To trim the shade, stencil some heart-with-leaves motifs around the bottom.

You can stencil and stitch a pair of bunny toys like the ones *above* in any size you like if you enlarge our patterns. (For speed and accuracy, use an enlarging photocopier.) Stencil the clothing and features first, then add embroidered outlines and accents, lace and ribbon trims, and tiny beads for eyes.

Bassinet

Shown on page 39.

MATERIALS
Basic stenciling and painting
  supplies
Wicker bassinet
Base coat for bassinet: ivory
  latex satin enamel
Stencil paints: Stencil Decor
  vanity teal and dusty rose, or
  suitable substitutes
Two contrasting fabrics: a print
  for skirt and dyed muslin (in
  a coordinating color) for ruffle
Water-erasable marking pen

INSTRUCTIONS
  Before beginning, see the Stenciling Primer, pages 74–79, for information on stenciling supplies, cutting stencils, and applying paint to stencil areas.
  Paint bassinet inside and out with two coats of ivory enamel, sanding lightly between coats.
  Make skirt for bassinet that reaches to the floor. Cut 20½-inch-deep ruffle; assemble ruffle after stenciling is completed.

To make the stencils
  Referring to full-size pattern, *below,* cut stencils A and B of large heart-and-leaves motif. Label stencils and transfer registration markings with a marker.

To stencil the design
  Practice stenciling on a fabric scrap first. With a water-erasable marking pen, draw a baseline along fabric strip that is 2 inches above hem of ruffle. Position stencil A along this line; tape in place. Stencil with rose. Repeat stencil A for border, spacing it evenly along fabric edge. Position and tape stencil B; stencil with teal.
  When all stenciling is completed, heat-set designs on the wrong side of fabric with a hot iron.
  Complete ruffle and attach to bassinet. Add other trims to bassinet as desired.

Rocking Chair

Shown on page 38.

MATERIALS
Basic stenciling and painting
  supplies
Rocking chair, sanded and ready
  for base coat
Base coat for chair: ivory latex
  satin enamel
Stencil paints: Stencil Decor
  vanity teal and dusty rose, or
  suitable substitutes
Chalk pencil
Polyurethane varnish

INSTRUCTIONS
  Before beginning, see the Stenciling Primer, pages 74–79, for information on stenciling supplies, cutting stencils, and applying paint to stencil areas.
  Paint the chair with two coats of enamel, sanding lightly between coats. On a piece of tracing paper, draw the outlines of chair surfaces that are large enough for stencils, such as top rail of chair back or arms.

To make the stencils
  Referring to the full-size patterns throughout this chapter, trace motifs onto outlines. Cut stencils. Label each stencil and transfer registration markings with a marker.

To stencil the design
  Use chalk pencil to mark positions of stencils on chair. Referring to projects in this chapter that use the particular stencils you've chosen, stencil designs.
  Seal with two coats of polyurethane varnish, sanding lightly between coats.

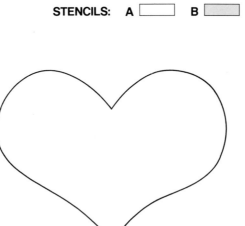

SMALL HEART-AND-LEAVES MOTIF
STENCILS: A ☐   **B** ▨

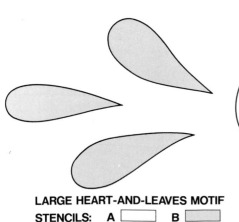
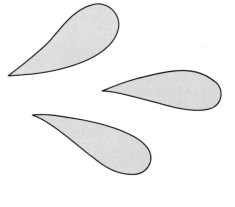

LARGE HEART-AND-LEAVES MOTIF
STENCILS: A ☐   **B** ☐

Bunny Toy Box

Shown on page 41.

Finished design is 9 inches high.

MATERIALS
Basic stenciling and painting
  supplies
Wooden toy box with hinged lid:
  Box shown is from Sears,
  Roebuck & Co.
Base coat for toy box: light
  green latex paint
Stencil paints: Stencil Decor
  genuine ivory, vanity teal, and
  dusty rose, or suitable
  substitutes
Brown permanent fine-point
  marker
Polyurethane varnish
Primer

INSTRUCTIONS
Before beginning, see the Stenciling Primer, pages 74–79, for information on stenciling supplies, cutting stencils, and applying paint to stencil areas.

Prime the toy box. Paint with two coats of light green latex paint, sanding lightly between coats.

(*Note:* Front of toy box shown is 14x35 inches. Before stenciling your toy box, measure its front and make any necessary adjustments in placement of motifs.)

To make the stencils
Referring to full-size patterns, pages 48–49, cut stencils A, B, and C of large mother-bunny and father-bunny figures. Cut stencils A, B, and C of basket motif, page 46. Cut stencil for picket fence, *above right*. Cut stencils A and B of large heart-and-leaves motif, *opposite*. Label each stencil and transfer registration markings with permanent marker.

To stencil the designs
BOX: With a pencil and ruler, lightly draw a line 2½ inches up from the bottom on the front and sides of the toy box. Position all stencils so their bottoms abut this line.

Position and tape stencil C of the basket motif, including the

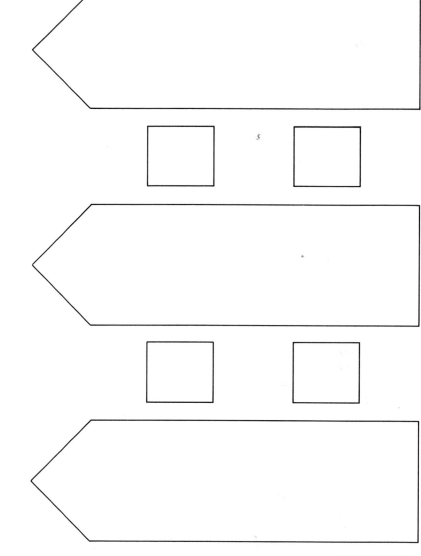

PICKET FENCE

bunny's ears, on the center front of the toy box; stencil with rose. Position and tape stencil A; stencil with ivory. Position and tape stencil B; stencil with teal.

Position the stencils for the mother bunny so her hand is about 1 inch to the basket's right (see photo, page 41). Tape stencil A in place and stencil with ivory.

Position and tape stencil B; stencil with teal. Position and tape stencil C; stencil with rose.

Position the stencils for the father bunny to the basket's left. Using stencils A, B, and C, stencil as for mother bunny.

Plan fence sections and spacing needed to fill the remaining areas along the front and sides of the box. Stencil the fence with ivory.

TOP RAIL: Plan position of large heart-and-leaves motif on top rail of toy box. This design is 2 inches high; omit or reduce this motif if your box has inadequate space for it.

Position and tape stencil A to rail; stencil with rose. Position and tape stencil B; stencil with teal.

When paint is dry, erase any pencil marks. Draw the bunny faces with a brown marker. Apply two coats of varnish, sanding lightly between coats.

BASKET MOTIF STENCILS:

A
B
C

To stencil the designs

Position and tape stencil B to each figure; stencil with rose.

Position and tape stencil C to each figure; stencil ears with rose. Stencil remaining areas of stencil C with teal.

When all paint is dry, draw the faces with a brown marker.

Spray with clear acrylic. Attach a picture hanger to the back of each figure.

Bunny Nursery Lamp

Shown on page 42.

Finished lamp is 10 inches tall, excluding the shade.

MATERIALS
Basic stenciling and painting
 supplies
Light green latex paint
Stencil paints: Stencil Decor
 genuine ivory, vanity teal, and
 dusty rose, or suitable
 substitutes
9-inch-diameter, 8-inch-high
 ivory lampshade
3/16-inch-diameter wood dowel
1x6x11-inch piece of pine (base)
½x6x9-inch piece of pine
 (pickets)
1x6x15-inch piece of pine
 (bunnies)
Two ¾x9-inch pieces of ¼-inch
 birch plywood (rails)
Cord set with molded plug and
 line switch
Keyless brass shell socket
8-inch-long, ⅛-inch brass rod
 for lamp fitting
Drill; ½-inch and 3/16-inch drill
 bits
Jigsaw; router
⅝-inch nails; hammer
Double-pointed tack
Four ½-inch-diameter round felt
 pads
Crafts glue
Brown permanent fine-point
 marker
Clear acrylic spray

Bunny Wall Decorations

Shown on page 40.

Bunnies are 9 inches tall.

MATERIALS
Basic stenciling and painting
 supplies
1x6x24-inch piece of pine
Stencil paints: Stencil Decor
 genuine ivory, vanity teal, and
 dusty rose, or suitable
 substitutes
Brown permanent fine-point
 marker
Band saw or jigsaw
Clear acrylic spray
2 sawtooth picture hangers

INSTRUCTIONS

Before beginning, see the Stenciling Primer, pages 74–79, for information on stenciling supplies, cutting stencils, and applying paint to stencil areas.

Referring to full-size patterns, pages 48–49, trace the outlines of the large mother-bunny and father-bunny figures. Transfer the patterns to pine and cut out the figures with a band saw or jigsaw.

Sand. Paint the bunnies with two coats of ivory, sanding lightly between coats.

To make the stencils

Cut stencils B and C of large bunny figures. Label each stencil and transfer registration markings with a permanent marker.

MEDIUM BUNNIES
STENCILS:

A
B
C

INSTRUCTIONS

Before beginning, see the Stenciling Primer, pages 74–79, for information on stenciling supplies, cutting stencils, and applying paint to stencil areas.

Referring to the full-size patterns, trace medium mother-bunny and father-bunny figures, *above,* and small fence picket, page 51. Transfer the patterns to pine. Cut out one of each of the figures and four of the pickets.

Round the edges of the base with a router. Drill a ½-inch-diameter hole through the center of the base. For dowels, drill ³/₁₆-inch-diameter holes into the center bottoms of the bunnies and two of the pickets. Sand wood pieces.

Lay the four pickets about 1 inch apart on a work surface, placing on the ends the pickets with the holes. Center and nail the bottom rail to the pickets, placing the bottom of the rail ³/₈ inch above the bottoms of the pickets. Nail the second rail so its bottom is ½ inch above the top of the bottom rail.

Position the bunnies about 1 inch from the front of the base; position the fence about 1¼ inches from the back of the base. Mark the base for the locations of the dowel holes. Drill ³/₁₆-inch-diameter holes at the marked locations. Paint the bunny figures with two coats of ivory, sanding lightly between coats. Paint the assembled fence with light green latex paint. Paint the base rose.

To make the stencils

Cut stencils B and C of medium mother-bunny and father-bunny figures, *above.* Cut stencils A and B of small heart-and-leaves motif, page 44. Label each stencil and transfer registration markings with permanent marker.

To stencil the designs

BUNNIES: Position and tape stencil B to figures; stencil with teal. Position and tape stencil C to figures; stencil with rose. Draw the faces with a brown marker.

LAMPSHADE: Mark position of six small heart-and-leaves motifs, evenly spaced, along bottom edge of lampshade. Position and tape stencil A about 1 inch above bottom edge; stencil with rose. Position and tape stencil B; stencil with teal.

continued

A BUNNY FAMILY FOR BABY'S ROOM

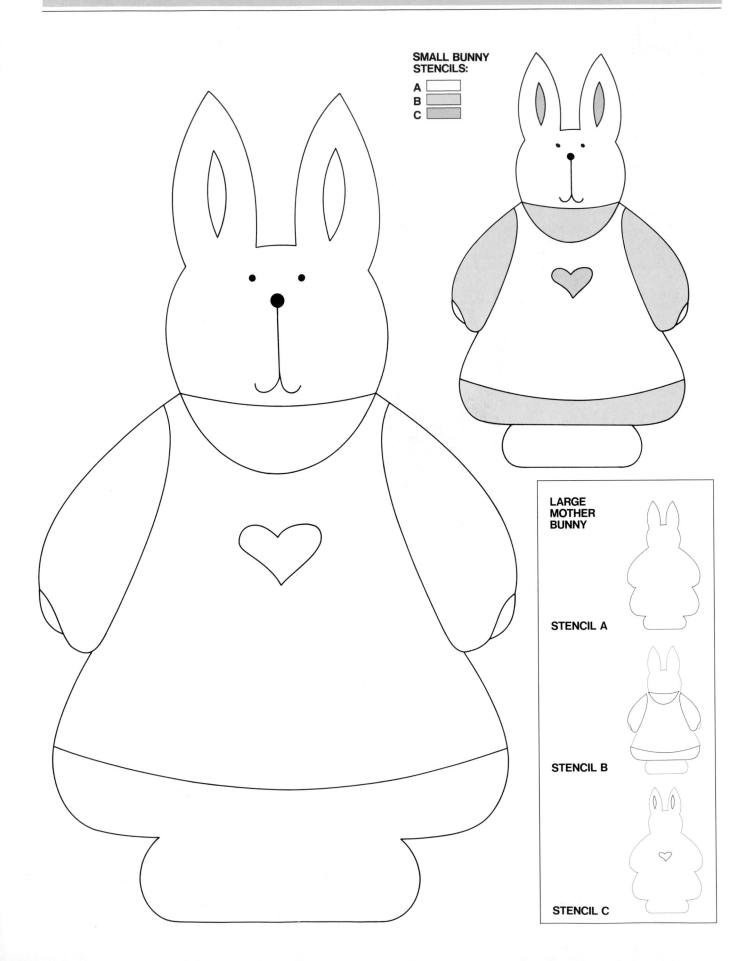

SMALL BUNNY
STENCILS:

A
B
C

LARGE
MOTHER
BUNNY

STENCIL A

STENCIL B

STENCIL C

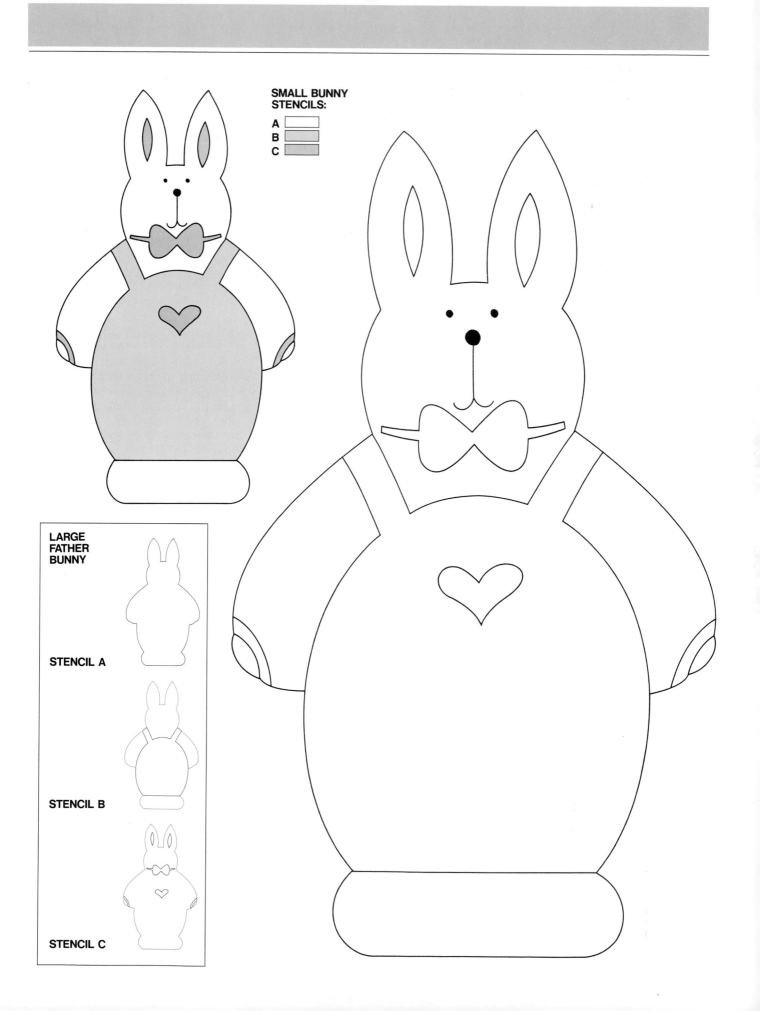

SMALL BUNNY
STENCILS:

A
B
C

LARGE
FATHER
BUNNY

STENCIL A

STENCIL B

STENCIL C

A BUNNY FAMILY FOR BABY'S ROOM

To assemble the lamp

Glue dowels to the bunnies and the fence, then to the base. Seal base with acrylic spray.

Fit the brass rod into the center of the base. Run the cord through the rod to the socket. Wire the socket to the cord; screw the socket into the rod. Pound a double-pointed tack over the cord to hold it flat against the bottom of the base. Glue felt pads to the base.

Bunny Peg Rack

Shown on page 42.

Finished rack is 8½x19 inches.

MATERIALS

Basic stenciling and painting supplies
Base coat for fence: light green latex paint
Stencil paints: Stencil Decor genuine ivory, vanity teal, and dusty rose, or suitable substitutes
Four 3-inch Shaker pegs
1x6x12-inch piece of pine (pickets)
Two ½x¾x19-inch pieces of pine (rails)
½x12x18-inch piece of pine (heart and bunnies)
Jigsaw; router; drill and ½-inch bit; hammer
⅞- and 1-inch nails
Brown permanent fine-point marker
Crafts glue
Clear acrylic spray

INSTRUCTIONS

Before beginning, see the Stenciling Primer, pages 74–79, for information on stenciling supplies, cutting stencils, and applying paint to stencil areas.

Referring to full-size patterns, pages 48–49, trace small mother-bunny and father-bunny figures. Transfer patterns to pine. Trace large fence picket and heart shape, *opposite,* and transfer to pine. Cut out one of each of the figures and four fence pickets. Cut out one large heart shape, curving top edge with a router. Paint the bunny figures with two

coats of ivory, sanding lightly between coats.

To make the stencils

Cut stencils B and C of small mother-bunny and father-bunny figures, pages 48–49. Label each stencil and transfer the registration markings with a permanent marker.

To stencil the designs

Position and tape stencil B to figures; stencil with teal. Position and tape stencil C to figures; stencil with rose. Draw the faces with a brown marker.

To assemble the rack

Drill a hole into center of each fence picket for a peg.

Lay the fence rails 1 inch apart on a work surface. Center heart on top; mark position and remove heart. Position inner pickets just adjacent to markings for heart and outer pickets ⅝ inch from the ends of the rails. The pickets on each side should be ⅝ inch apart. Using 1-inch nails, nail the pickets to the rails.

Glue a peg in each picket hole.

Paint fence with two coats of light green latex paint, sanding lightly between coats. Paint the heart rose.

Glue the bunny figures to the front of the heart. Glue and nail the heart to the fence.

Seal rack with acrylic spray.

Bunny Toys

Shown on page 43.

Finished size is 7½x12¼ inches.

MATERIALS

Basic stenciling supplies
½ yard of unbleached muslin
Stencil paints: Stencil Decor vanity teal and dusty rose, or suitable substitutes
Polyester fiberfill
Embroidery floss: One skein *each* of teal, dusty rose, and dark brown
Four dark brown seed beads
Two ¼-inch-diameter white buttons; needle; white thread

Scraps of lace; ⅛-inch dusty rose satin ribbon
Water-erasable marking pen

INSTRUCTIONS

Before beginning, see the Stenciling Primer, pages 74–79, for information on stenciling supplies, cutting stencils, and applying paint to stencil areas.

Preshrink muslin, press, and set aside.

To stencil the designs

Referring to patterns, pages 48–49, trace large mother-bunny and father-bunny figures. Using a photocopier with enlargement capabilities, enlarge patterns until each outline is 12 inches high.

Cut stencils for father bunny. Following manufacturer's instructions for stenciling onto muslin, stencil overalls onto muslin with teal; stencil paws, bow tie, ears, and heart with rose. Cut stencils for mother bunny. Stencil ears, dress hem, neckline, and sleeves with rose; stencil heart with teal. Heat-set colors on the wrong side of the fabric with a hot iron.

Using three plies of floss and working in outline stitch, embroider around father bunny and his overalls with teal floss. Satin-stitch paws, ears, bow tie, and heart with dusty rose floss. Sew two white buttons beneath overalls straps.

Outline-stitch around mother bunny, dress, and paws with dusty rose floss; satin-stitch ears with dusty rose floss and heart with teal floss. Sew lace trim around neckline; thread ribbon through lace and tie into bow.

Embroider faces on bunnies with dark brown floss. Add two beads for eyes.

To assemble the toys

With water-erasable marking pen on wrong side of fabric, draw outlines of bunnies ¼ inch beyond stitched outlines. Place right sides of muslin backing and stenciled fabric together. Stitch along line, leaving an opening at bottom. Trim to ¼ inch beyond stitching, clip curves, and turn. Stuff and close.

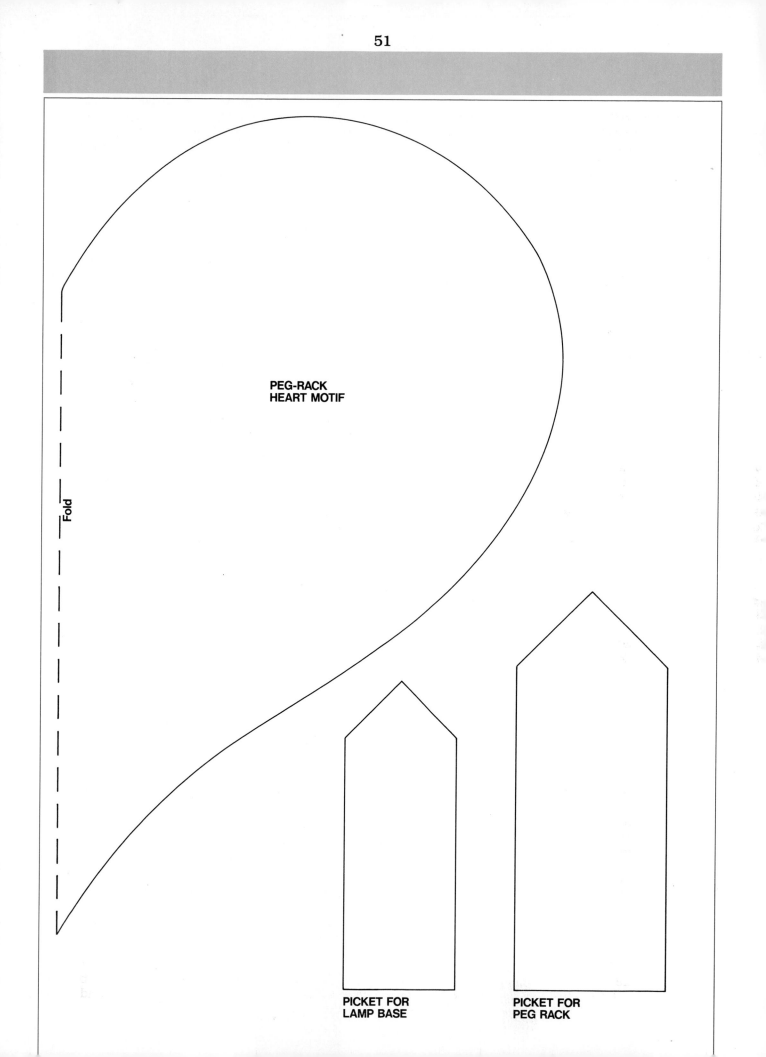

**PEG-RACK
HEART MOTIF**

Fold

**PICKET FOR
LAMP BASE**

**PICKET FOR
PEG RACK**

PERSONAL TOUCHES

FOR YOUR HOME

It's the finishing touches that turn a house into a home, and using handcrafted accessories is a sure way to add a country feel to your surroundings. The stenciled projects in this chapter are tailor-made for those searching for one-of-a-kind accents just right for every room in a country home, from kitchen to living and dining areas to playroom.

The schoolhouse, trees, picket fence, and other stenciled motifs, *right* and *opposite,* can be put to good use in a variety of ways. We've chosen to decorate a set of four unfinished canisters with a country landscape.

Because your set of canisters may be a different size from ours, it's best to begin with a drawing that adapts our patterns to fit your canisters. Do that by first drawing a rectangle that corresponds to the front of each canister. Then, using the full-size patterns that appear on pages 62–63, compose a portion of the landscape on each canister.

To make the most of these motifs, you might stencil the fence and other items above a kitchen counter, along a chair rail, or on a splashboard in the bathroom.

To stencil a cutting board like the one *opposite,* center a large tree on the painted side and trim with flowers and a checkerboard border.

Instructions and patterns for the projects in this chapter begin on page 62.

With a few adaptations, some of the smaller motifs from the projects on the previous pages succeed all by themselves. The bread box, *above,* uses a smaller version of the flower motif and several rows of the checkerboard pattern. Alternate rows of flowers and checks to fit your container, or devise your own design.

Keep in mind that, if you're stenciling an object with different dimensions from ours, it's best to work out the positions of the motifs on paper before beginning to stencil.

The floorcloth, *opposite,* features an enlarged version of the schoolhouse from the canister set on pages 52–53. A grid of stripes and squares forms the basis for placing the remaining motifs: a graceful vine and simple three-leaf design. We recommend several coats of polyurethane varnish to prevent paint from chipping off the floorcloth's surface.

Stenciling was particularly popular during the 19th century, when lavish ornamentation covering large areas was fashionable. These projects reflect some of the characteristics of this period: bird and floral motifs, allover patterns, and the combining of elements of varying scale.

The blanket chest, *left*, features flower-decorated arches surrounding bird motifs. One flower from the bird's branch is repeated for the floorcloth, *left*. Stencil just a single bird and its accompanying flowers atop a cheesebox, *opposite* and *below*.

F or a charming accessory in a kids room, stencil a large checkerboard onto the center of a 37-inch-diameter table, *opposite.* Draw accurate centerlines to position the first elements, and the remaining stencil motifs will fall into place.

Checks—a mainstay of country-style decoration—are easy to stencil, one row at a time. In fact, stenciling checks is the best way to assure crisp, even squares.

Surround the checkerboard with motifs from a farm landscape: a house, a barn, rolling hills, an apple orchard, and chickens, cows, and sheep. To repeat the soft accents shown *above,* use light brushstrokes to fill in grassy areas and create clouds in the sky.

For checkers, paint unfinished wooden apples in two colors; add felt leaves to create "kings."

PERSONAL TOUCHES

Stenciling is such a fast and inexpensive craft that it's fun (and practical) to decorate everyday objects. The designs on the flowerpots, *above,* offer a few suggestions for using some of the patterns in this book in imaginative ways. With the exception of the ropelike border motif, all of the motifs are borrowed from the designs on the jelly cupboard, *opposite.*

The cupboard has a design on each section of its raised-panel door. A vine pattern—which is just one stencil reversed and repeated— forms the symmetrical border. The stenciling on the inside of the bowl, *opposite,* echoes the motif from the cupboard door.

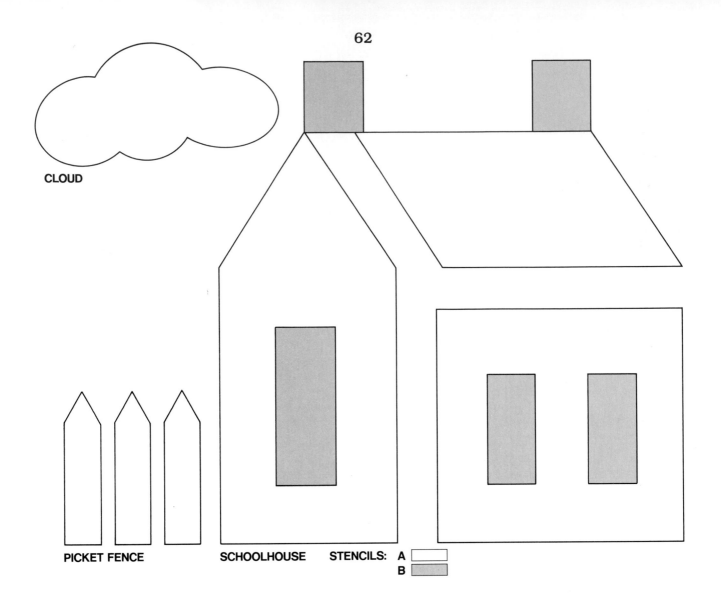

CLOUD

PICKET FENCE   SCHOOLHOUSE   STENCILS: A
                                          B

Canister Set

Shown on pages 52–53.

MATERIALS
Basic stenciling and painting supplies
Set of four unfinished wooden canisters
Base coat for canisters: light blue-gray latex paint
Stencil paints: antique white, medium green, light green, rust, medium blue, and medium yellow
Polyurethane varnish

INSTRUCTIONS
Before beginning, see the Stenciling Primer, pages 74–79, for information on stenciling supplies, cutting stencils, and applying paint to stencil areas.

Paint sides and lids of canisters with two coats of light blue-gray paint, sanding lightly between coats. Using medium green, paint a 1-inch strip around the bottom of each canister. Align all motifs (except flowers) along this line.

To make the stencils
Referring to full-size patterns, *above* and *opposite,* cut stencils for picket fence, large tree, small tree, large flower and stem-and-leaf design, cloud, and stencils A and B of schoolhouse. Label each stencil and transfer any registration markings with a marker.

To stencil the designs
Refer to photograph of canisters, pages 52–53. Keeping a picket flush to front edge, stencil a picket fence along each side of each canister with antique white.

LARGE CANISTER: Stencil a large tree on left side of canister front using medium green. Stencil a small tree on right side using light green. Stencil a few antique white pickets on front. Stencil two stem-and-leaf designs using

light green; stencil medium blue and rust flowers above stems.

MEDIUM-LARGE CANISTER: Position and tape stencil A of schoolhouse motif flush to right side of canister front; stencil with rust. Position and tape stencil B of schoolhouse motif; stencil chimneys with rust and windows with light blue-gray latex paint. Add a few pickets; add medium yellow and medium blue flowers.

MEDIUM-SMALL CANISTER: Stencil a picket fence across front. Stencil two clouds with antique white. Add four colored flowers.

SMALL CANISTER: Stencil a small tree with light green. Add some fence pickets and a flower.

When all stenciling is completed, seal with two coats of polyurethane varnish, sanding lightly between coats.

PERSONAL TOUCHES FOR YOUR HOME

Cutting Board

Shown on page 53.

MATERIALS
Basic stenciling and painting
   supplies
Unfinished cutting board
Base coat for board: light blue-
   gray latex paint
Stencil paints: antique white,
   medium green, light green,
   medium blue, rust, and
   medium yellow
Polyurethane varnish

INSTRUCTIONS
   Before beginning, see the Stenciling Primer, pages 74–79, for information on stenciling supplies,
cutting stencils, and applying
paint to stencil areas.
   Paint one flat side and all edges
of cutting board with two coats of
light blue-gray latex paint, sanding lightly between coats. (The
cutting surface of any breadboard
or cutting board should never be
painted.)

To make the stencils
   Referring to the full-size patterns, cut stencils for large tree
and for large flower and stem-
and-leaf design, *right;* cut stencil
for checkerboard, page 64. Label
each stencil and transfer any registration markings with a permanent marker.

To stencil the designs
   Stencil a 1-inch-wide checkerboard border around edge of cutting board with antique white;
keeping checks aligned, extend
pattern up handle.
   Position and tape the large tree
stencil in center of board; stencil
with medium green.
   Plan position of three flowers
near tree trunk. Position and tape
one stem-and-leaf design; stencil
stem and leaf with light green and
flower with medium blue. Repeat
twice more using rust and medium yellow for flowers.
   Apply two coats of polyurethane varnish, sanding lightly between coats.

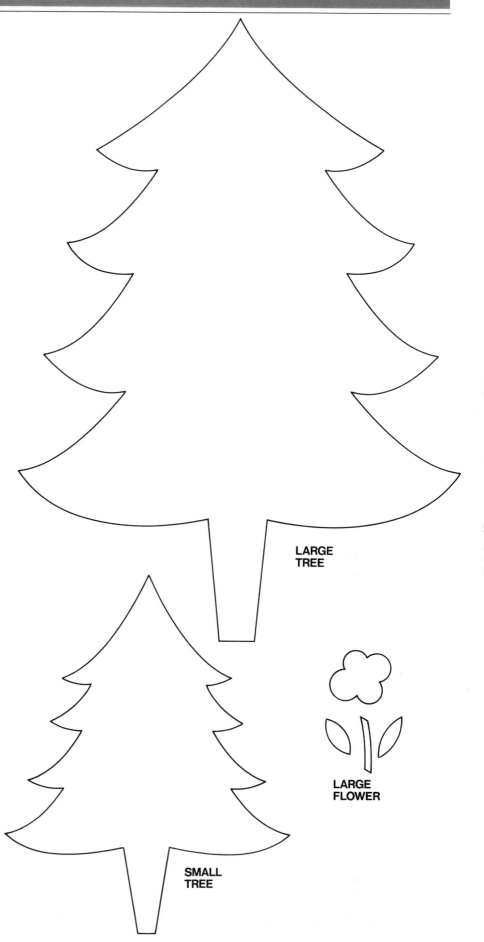

LARGE
TREE

SMALL
TREE

LARGE
FLOWER

PERSONAL TOUCHES FOR YOUR HOME

Bread Box

Shown on page 54.

MATERIALS
Basic stenciling and painting supplies
Unfinished bread box
Base coats for bread box: light blue-gray and antique white latex paints
Stencil paints: antique white, light green, medium green, medium blue, medium yellow, and rust
Polyurethane varnish

INSTRUCTIONS
Before beginning, see the Stenciling Primer, pages 74–79, for information on stenciling supplies, cutting stencils, and applying paint to stencil areas.

(*Note:* The bread box shown is only one of many styles appropriate for stenciling. Use the motifs shown or incorporate any of the patterns from pages 62–63. Make a tissue overlay of your completed design and stencil as desired.)

Paint top and front of bread box with two coats of light blue-gray latex paint, sanding lightly between coats. Paint sides and exposed bottom with two coats of antique white latex paint, sanding as above.

To make the stencils
Referring to the full-size patterns, *above right,* cut stencils of checkerboard and of small flower and stem-and-leaf design. For variety, cut two or three separate flower stencils, altering their shape slightly and using them randomly.

To stencil the designs
Box shown has eight slats. Stencil the top two, bottom two, and middle two with checks using antique white, medium yellow, and light green stencil paints. On the remaining slats stencil a row of medium green small stem-and-leaf motifs. Above each stem, stencil a flower using medium blue and rust.

Seal with two coats of varnish, sanding lightly between coats.

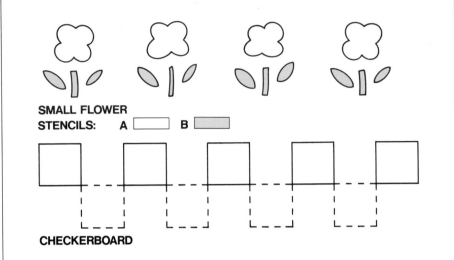

SMALL FLOWER STENCILS: A ☐   B ▭

CHECKERBOARD

Schoolhouse Floorcloth

Shown on page 55.

Finished size is 38x62 inches.

MATERIALS
Basic stenciling and painting supplies
42x66-inch piece of artist's canvas
Water-base primer
Base coat for canvas: antique white latex paint
Stencil paints: antique white, tan, brown, light green, dark green, barn red, and gold
Piece of plywood at least as large as canvas
Crafts glue
Staple gun; staples
Chalk pencil
Polyurethane varnish

INSTRUCTIONS
Before beginning, see the Stenciling Primer, pages 74–79, for information on stenciling supplies, cutting stencils, and applying paint to stencil areas.

Most canvas is sold from rolls to prevent creasing. If your canvas does have creases, press them with a hot iron.

Lay canvas on plywood. Pull the canvas taut and staple its edges to the plywood; be sure to place the staples within 1 inch of the edges.

Paint canvas with two coats of primer, sanding lightly between coats. Paint with two coats of antique white latex paint, sanding as above.

To paint the borders
With chalk pencil, outline finished size of rug: 38x62 inches. Within this space, mark a 2-inch-wide border on all four sides. Mark two strips down the length of the rug; mark four strips across the width of the rug. Make each strip 2 inches wide, and space the strips 10 inches apart. The completed design will have fifteen 10x10-inch squares, bordered by 2x10-inch strips.

Mask the 2x10-inch strips that abut the sides of the 10-inch squares; design shown has 38 such strips. Paint each strip tan. Carefully remove the masking. Then mask the twenty-four 2x2-inch squares at the corners of the 10-inch squares; paint the small squares gold.

To make the stencils
Referring to the full-size patterns, cut stencils A and B of the schoolhouse motif, page 62; cut stencils A, B, and C of the vine motif, *opposite;* cut stencils A and B of the center-vine motif, *opposite.* Label each stencil and transfer registration markings with a permanent marker.

To stencil the designs
In each 2x10-inch strip, position and tape stencil A of vine motif; stencil with brown. Position and tape stencil B of vine motif; stencil with dark green. Position

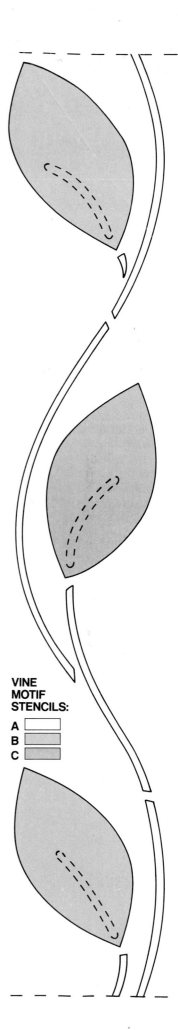

and tape stencil C of vine motif; stencil with light green. With a small paintbrush and brown, paint a small curved vein in the center of each leaf.

In the 10x10-inch corner squares, position and tape stencil A of the schoolhouse motif at a 45-degree angle; stencil with barn red. Position and tape stencil B. Stencil chimneys with barn red and windows with antique white stencil paint.

In alternating 10x10-inch squares, position and tape stencil A of center-vine motif; stencil with dark green. Position and tape stencil B of center-vine motif; stencil with brown.

To finish the floorcloth

Allow paint to cure for three to four days. Then apply one coat of varnish and let dry.

Remove staples from canvas. Measure and mark 1 inch past completed design; cut along this line. Turn canvas over. Cut the corners at 45-degree angles. Apply glue to canvas edges. Fold unpainted edges of canvas over, taking care to miter corners neatly. Weight the canvas while the glue sets and let dry overnight.

Turn canvas over and apply a second coat of varnish.

Flower-Patterned Floorcloth

Shown on pages 56–57.

Finished size is 55½x55½ inches.

MATERIALS
Basic stenciling and painting supplies
60x60-inch piece of artist's canvas
Water-base primer
Base coat for canvas: tan latex paint
Stencil paints: barn red, forest green, and black
Scrap 2x4s or scraps of plywood
Staple gun; staples; crafts glue
Chalk pencil
Polyurethane varnish

continued

VINE MOTIF STENCILS:

A
B
C

CENTER-VINE MOTIF STENCILS:

A
B

PERSONAL TOUCHES FOR YOUR HOME

INSTRUCTIONS

Before beginning, see the Stenciling Primer, pages 74–79, for information on stenciling supplies, cutting stencils, and applying paint to stencil areas.

Most canvas is sold from rolls to prevent creasing. If your canvas does have creases, press them with a hot iron.

Construct a wooden frame from scrap 2x4s to size of canvas; or connect two pieces of plywood with wooden braces. Pull the canvas taut and staple its edges to frame; be sure to place the staples within 1 inch of the edges.

Paint canvas with two coats of primer, sanding lightly between coats. Paint with two coats of tan latex paint, sanding as above.

To make the stencils

Referring to full-size patterns, cut stencils for floorcloth motif, *right,* and the two floorcloth-border motifs, *opposite.* Label each stencil and transfer registration markings with a marker.

To paint the borders

With chalk pencil, mark finished size of 55½x55½ inches. Mark and mask the first border 2½ inches in on all four sides; paint this border barn red. Mark and mask next border ¾ inch farther in; paint it forest green. Mark a border 3¾ inches farther in; leave it tan. Mark and mask last border ¾ inch farther in; paint it forest green. Remaining center design area is 40x40 inches.

To stencil the designs

Make a tissue overlay to fit 3¾-inch-wide tan border. Trace floorcloth-border motifs, alternating each design to create pattern. Position and tape stencils along border; stencil with black.

In middle of floorcloth, mark horizontal and vertical centerlines. *Lightly* pencil a grid with lines spaced 1½ inches apart. Using floorcloth motif and barn red, stencil the allover pattern, aligning centers of flowers with intersections on grid.

When all stenciling is completed and paint is *thoroughly dry,* erase penciled grid marks.

To finish the floorcloth

Finish as for the Schoolhouse Floorcloth; instructions begin on page 64.

Blanket Chest

Shown on pages 56–57.

Arch motif is 11x11¾ inches.

MATERIALS

Basic stenciling and painting supplies
New or antique chest
Base coats for chest: forest green and barn red latex paints
Stencil paints: barn red, black, medium green, medium blue, and medium yellow
Polyurethane varnish

INSTRUCTIONS

Before beginning, see the Stenciling Primer, pages 74–79, for information on stenciling supplies, cutting stencils, and applying paint to stencil areas.

If chest is painted, strip paint from front surface; strip remaining surfaces or sand thoroughly.

Referring to full-size pattern of bird border, pages 68–69, trace arched shape.

Make a tissue overlay of chest front. Plan placement of two arches, each surrounding a bird motif, page 68. Trace arched shapes onto front of chest. (*Note:* The center design on the chest shown is a feature of that chest.) Mask the area with tape and nonporous paper, and paint the chest with two coats of forest green latex paint, sanding lightly between coats. Paint legs and rim of lid with two coats of barn red latex paint, sanding as above. Remove masking. Paint a 1¼-inch-wide barn-red-latex-paint border within each arch. Area inside arches behind birds remains unpainted.

FLOORCLOTH MOTIF

To make the stencils

Referring to the full-size patterns, pages 68–69, cut stencils for both sides of the bird-border motif. Cut stencils A, B, C, and D of the bird motif. Label each stencil and transfer registration markings with a marker.

To stencil the designs

Following the placement shown on bird-border pattern, pages 68–69, stencil designs onto borders with black. Following the instructions for the Cheesebox, page 70, stencil the bird motif within one of the arches.

Reverse stencils to paint the bird motif facing the opposite direction in the other arch. Allow stencils to dry thoroughly before turning them over.

Seal all painted surfaces with two coats of varnish, sanding lightly between coats.

FLOORCLOTH-BORDER MOTIFS

Match Line AB

A

B

BIRD MOTIF
STENCILS:

A
B
C
D

Match Line AB

A

B

BIRD-BORDER MOTIF

BIRD
PLACEMENT

Fold

Match Line

PERSONAL TOUCHES FOR YOUR HOME

Cheesebox

Shown on page 57.

MATERIALS
Basic stenciling and painting
 supplies
12-inch-diameter cheesebox
Base coats for box: barn red and
 forest green latex paints
Stencil paints: barn red, black,
 medium green, medium blue,
 and medium yellow
Polyurethane varnish

INSTRUCTIONS
 Before beginning, see the Stenciling Primer, pages 74–79, for information on stenciling supplies,
cutting stencils, and applying paint to stencil areas.
 Paint bottom of box with two coats of forest green latex paint, sanding lightly between coats. Paint rim of lid and handle similarly with barn red. Leave top of box unfinished.

To make the stencils
 Referring to full-size pattern, page 68, cut stencils A, B, C, and D of bird motif. Label each stencil and transfer registration markings with a permanent marker.

To stencil the designs
 Position and tape stencil A on lid; stencil with barn red. Position and tape stencil B; stencil with
medium green. Position and tape stencil C; stencil with medium blue. Position and tape stencil D. Mask flower centers and stencil remaining areas with black; remove masking and stencil flower centers with medium yellow.
 Seal with two coats of varnish.

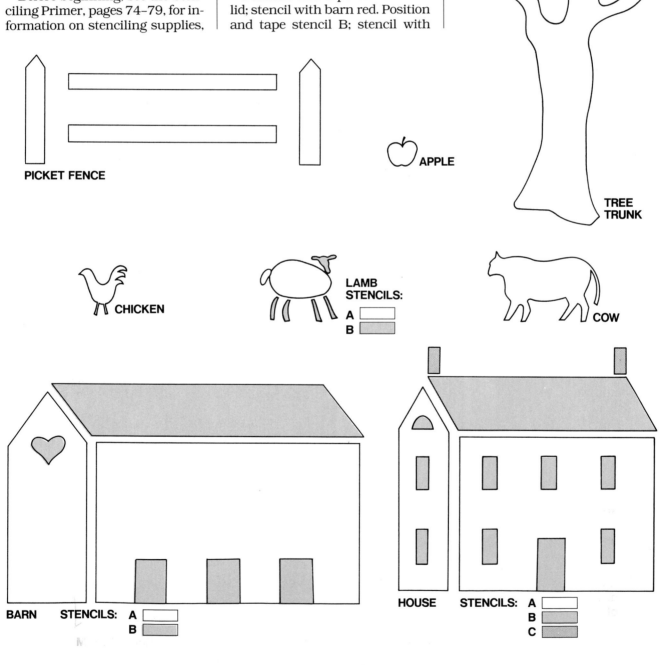

PICKET FENCE

APPLE

TREE TRUNK

CHICKEN

LAMB STENCILS:
A
B

COW

BARN   STENCILS: A
                   B

HOUSE   STENCILS: A
                    B
                    C

Barnyard Checker Table

Shown on pages 58–59.

MATERIALS
Basic stenciling and painting supplies
Child-height table with 37-inch-diameter top
Base coat for table legs: barn red latex enamel
Base coat for tabletop: off-white latex paint
Stencil paints: barn red, yellow ocher, forest green, colonial blue, ultramarine blue, burnt umber, black, and white
Medium brown antiquing liquid; soft rag
24 wooden apples
Green felt; needle and thread
Chalk pencil
Polyurethane varnish

INSTRUCTIONS
Before beginning, see the Stenciling Primer, pages 74–79, for information on stenciling supplies, cutting stencils, and applying paint to stencil areas.

Sand the tabletop; wipe with a tack cloth. Paint tabletop with two coats of off-white latex paint, sanding lightly between coats.

Paint the edge of the tabletop with forest green. To create the scalloped edge around the perimeter of the tabletop, use forest green and a 1-inch stencil brush. Holding the stencil brush half on and half off the edge, gently bounce the brush along the edge and make half-circles that slightly overlap.

Find exact center of tabletop and mark with a dot using chalk pencil. Then draw horizontal and vertical centerlines and two 45-degree diagonal lines.

To make the stencils
Referring to full-size patterns, *opposite,* cut stencils A and B of barn and stencils A, B, and C of house. Cut single stencils of fence, apple-tree trunk, apple, chicken, and cow. Cut stencils A and B of lamb. For checkerboard stencil, draw four 1½x1½-inch squares, placed in a row and spaced 1½ inches apart, onto stencil material. Cut squares.

Label each stencil and transfer any necessary registration markings with permanent marker.

To stencil the designs
CHECKERBOARD: Draw a line 6 inches below horizontal centerline. Place bottom edge of checkerboard stencil along chalk line. Tape in place and stencil with barn red stencil paint. Remove and reverse stencil so that painted and unpainted squares are offset; place bottom edge of row along top edge of squares just stenciled and repeat. Repeat this pattern until there are eight rows of checkerboard squares. Checkerboard area should measure 12x12 inches when completed.

BUILDINGS: Position and tape stencil A of the barn along vertical centerline 3 inches from the edge of the table; stencil with barn red stencil paint. Position and tape stencil B; stencil with black. Repeat on the opposite side of the table.

Position and tape stencil A of house along horizontal centerline 3 inches from edge of the table; stencil with colonial blue. Position and tape stencil B of house; stencil with black. Position and tape stencil C; stencil with barn red stencil paint. Repeat house on opposite side of table.

FENCES: Position and tape stencil A of fence 1½ inches from edge of table along one diagonal line; stencil with white. Repeat on remaining diagonal lines.

APPLE TREES: Position and tape stencil A of tree trunk ½ inch to the right of each fence; stencil with burnt umber. Reverse stencil; position and tape ½ inch to the left of each fence and stencil with burnt umber.

To create leaves on the trees, dip a ½-inch stencil brush into forest green, dabbing out the excess; then dip the left side of the brush into ultramarine blue. Keeping the blue edge of the brush to the left, bounce the brush until the trees are covered. Using apple stencil, position and tape apples randomly over the trees (position one on the ground near each tree); stencil with barn red stencil paint.

GRASS: With chalk pencil, lightly sketch a curving line from the bases of the fences to the bases of the buildings. Using forest green, bounce a ½-inch stencil brush lightly along chalked line. Making short brushstrokes, lightly shade the areas below the grass with forest green and yellow ocher.

SKY AND SMOKE: With colonial blue, make small streaks above the buildings and between the trees. Mix a small amount of black and white paint; bounce brush to make small puffs above each chimney.

ANIMALS: With barn red stencil paint, stencil three chickens to the lower left of one of the barns; reverse one of the chickens. With black, stencil two cows to lower right of barn. Repeat below barn on opposite side. Position stencil A of lamb in front of one of the houses; stencil with white. Position stencil B of lamb; stencil with black. Repeat twice more in front of this house. Repeat all three in front of house on opposite side.

Remove chalk with a damp rag.

Apply antiquing liquid with a soft rag. Let dry. Apply two coats of polyurethane varnish, sanding lightly betwen coats.

Paint legs and underside of table with barn red latex enamel.

APPLES: Using stencil paints, paint 12 apples red and 12 apples green to use as checkers. Cut leaf shapes, *below,* from green felt. Fold leaves in half; sew or glue leaves together, leaving stems open. To add a "king" to a checker, slip a leaf over the apple stem.

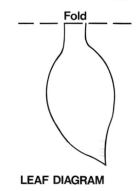

LEAF DIAGRAM

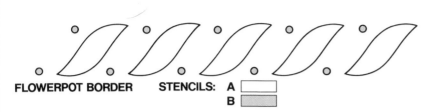

FLOWERPOT BORDER **STENCILS: A** ☐ **B** ▨

Jelly Cupboard

Shown on page 61.

MATERIALS
Basic stenciling and painting
   supplies
Jelly cupboard
Base coats for cupboard: antique
   white and rust latex paints
Stencil paints: rust, medium
   yellow, medium blue, and
   medium green
Chalk pencil
Polyurethane varnish

INSTRUCTIONS
   Before beginning, see the Stenciling Primer, pages 74–79, for information on stenciling supplies, cutting stencils, and applying paint to stencil areas.
   Paint sides and front of cupboard with two coats of antique white latex paint, sanding lightly between coats. Paint top, molding, side trim, and outline of door with rust latex paint, sanding lightly between coats. Paint inside of cupboard as desired. With chalk pencil, mark centerlines of door panels.

To make the stencils
   Referring to full-size patterns, *opposite,* cut stencils A, B, C, and D of cupboard motif; cut stencil of cupboard-border motif. Label each stencil and transfer registration markings with a permanent marker.

To stencil the designs
DOORS: Position and tape stencil A of cupboard motif on one door panel; stencil with medium blue. Repeat on second panel.
   Position and tape stencil B; stencil with medium green.

   Position and tape stencil C; stencil with medium yellow.
   Position and tape stencil D; stencil with rust stencil paint.

   BORDER: Beginning at top, position and tape stencil for cupboard border to one side of cupboard; stencil with rust stencil paint. Remove stencil and reverse; continue to stencil motifs along side (see photo, page 61). Repeat for other side of cupboard, positioning stencils to form a mirror image of other side.
   Paint centers of border flowers freehand with medium yellow.
   Seal cupboard with two coats of polyurethane varnish.

Flowerpots

Shown on page 60.

MATERIALS
Basic stenciling and painting
   supplies
Clay flowerpots: Two 5¾-inch-
   diameter (at top), 5¼-inch-
   high pots and one 8¾-inch-
   diameter, 6½-inch-high pot
Base coats for pots: antique
   white, rust, and medium blue
   latex paints
Stencil paints: antique white,
   rust, medium blue, medium
   green, and medium yellow.
Chalk pencil
Polyurethane varnish

INSTRUCTIONS
   Before beginning, see the Stenciling Primer, pages 74–79, for information on stenciling supplies, cutting stencils, and applying paint to stencil areas.
   Paint one of the small pots with rust latex paint; paint the other

with medium blue latex paint. Paint the lower section of the large pot with rust latex paint; paint the rim with antique white latex paint.

To make the stencils
   Referring to the full-size patterns, *opposite,* cut a stencil of the flower from the cupboard-border motif; cut stencils A, B, and C of the center flower from the cupboard motif. Cut stencils A and B of the flowerpot-border motif, *left.* Label each stencil and transfer any registration markings with a permanent marker.

To stencil the designs
   SMALL RUST POT: With chalk pencil, divide the lower surface into four equal parts. Using the leaves only from stencil B of the cupboard motif, stencil along each chalked line with medium green. Using the flower stencil from the cupboard motif, stencil a flower in the center of each leaf cluster with antique white stencil paint. Using the same stencil, stencil two flowers between each cluster of leaves with antique white stencil paint, one above and one below the green leaves. Stencil the flowerpot-border motif along the rim, using medium green for the leaves and antique white stencil paint for the dots.

   SMALL BLUE POT: Using flower portion from cupboard-border motif only, randomly stencil flowers around pot with antique white, rust, and medium yellow stencil paints. Paint centers freehand with medium yellow and antique white stencil paints.

   LARGE POT: With a chalk pencil, divide the lower surface of the pot into eight equal parts. Using the central flower design from the cupboard motif, stencil A, B, and C with medium blue, medium green, and medium yellow as for Jelly Cupboard (see instructions, *left*). Stencil rim with flowerpot-border motif, using medium blue for both stencils.
   Seal each flowerpot with two coats of varnish, sanding lightly between coats.

Bowl

Shown on page 61.

MATERIALS

Basic stenciling and painting
   supplies
12-inch-diameter (at top)
   unfinished wooden bowl
Base coat for bowl: medium
   yellow latex paint
Stencil paints: medium green,
   antique white, and rust
Polyurethane varnish

INSTRUCTIONS

Before beginning, see the Stenciling Primer, pages 74–79, for information on stenciling supplies, cutting stencils, and applying paint to stencil areas.

Paint inside of bowl with two coats of medium yellow latex paint, sanding lightly between coats. Leave outside of bowl unpainted. Mark center of inside of bowl with a small dot.

To make the stencils

Referring to full-size pattern, *right,* cut stencils A, B, C, and D of cupboard motif; cut a stencil of just the flower from cupboard-border motif. Label each stencil and transfer registration markings with a permanent marker.

To stencil the designs

Position and tape stencil A of cupboard motif inside bowl, centering it on dot; stencil with antique white. Keeping stencil aligned with center dot, turn stencil a quarter-turn; stencil again with antique white. Position and tape stencil B of cupboard motif; stencil with medium green in both places. Position and tape stencil C of cupboard motif; stencil with antique white in both places. Position and tape stencil D of cupboard motif; stencil with antique white in both places. Stencil flower center with rust. Position and tape flower stencil from cupboard-border motif midway between stenciled areas; stencil with antique white.

Seal with two coats of varnish.

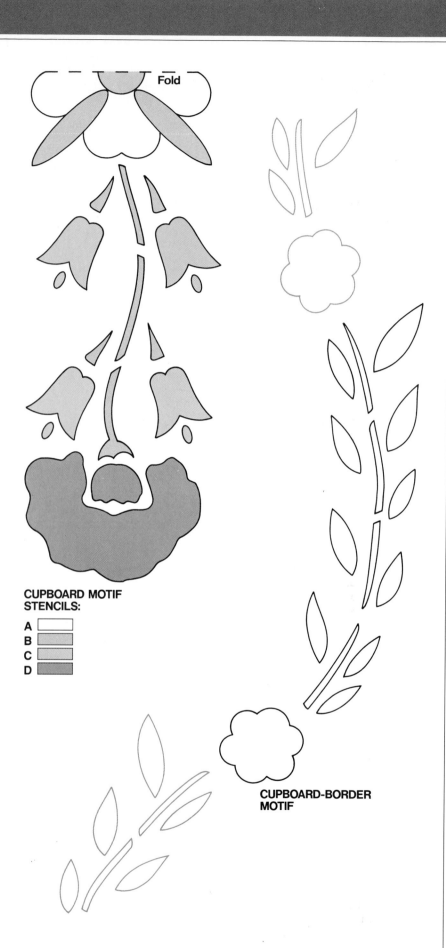

Fold

**CUPBOARD MOTIF
STENCILS:**

A
B
C
D

**CUPBOARD-BORDER
MOTIF**

Although the craft of stenciling has been used to create surface decoration for centuries, the technique has for the most part remained unchanged.

Here and on the next five pages is an overview of basic stenciling supplies and equipment, as well as a look at how to cut and use stencils, how to apply paint to stencil areas, and how to combine several stencils to create one design.

Materials

With the exception of brushes and acetate sheets, most of the materials and equipment required for stenciling are the same as those used for any other decorative-painting technique. The materials suggested for the projects in this book are available at crafts- and art-supply shops or at paint and hardware stores.

Stencil brushes

As with many other painting techniques, stenciling requires its own type of brush. Stencil brushes are designed to hold a minimum of pigment and, when used properly, to apply paint to flat areas evenly and smoothly.

Although stencil brushes come in various sizes, they all are similarly made. The bristles are gathered into a circular shape at the end of the brush's shaft, and are trimmed bluntly across the end. Because brushes are used in an up-and-down motion, only the ends of the bristles come into contact with the paint and the stenciled area.

The best stencil brushes are made with natural hog bristles. Dark bristles are more pliable and have more uses; brittle light-colored bristles are best suited for larger projects.

The one advantage of synthetic-bristled brushes over the natural-bristled ones is that the synthetic brushes are less expensive. Brushes that have a small sponge instead of bristles are even cheaper, but they're suitable for one-time use only.

Always clean a brush with warm soapy water after use, and rinse thoroughly. Keep a wide selection of brushes handy; many stencilers use one brush for each color of paint.

Stencil material

In the past, stencil artists were required to cut stencils from thin metal plates or heavy paper. These stencils were durable and easy to create, but, because they were opaque, they were difficult to position accurately.

Today, the widespread availability of clear acetate sheets has enabled stencil artists to design and cut their own stencils efficiently and inexpensively. Clear acetate sheets are not only easy to cut (and repair if they are torn), but they let the stencil artist see exactly where the stenciled area is positioned.

Acetate is available at crafts- and art-supply shops; buy it by the sheet or from rolls.

Many shops that specialize in stenciling supplies also offer stencil blanks. These sheets are often translucent acetate, and sometimes are embossed with a textured surface that clings better to painted objects than artist's acetate does.

Stencils cut from acetate will last indefinitely and can be used over and over. Store stencils in a flat box; place sheets of tissue paper between the stencils.

Paints

The projects in this book require two types of paint: latex paint for the base coat and stencil paints.

Water-soluble latex paint is available at paint and hardware stores.

Paints suitable for stenciling can come from a variety of sources. Artist's acrylic paints, which come in either tubes or small jars, work well when properly thinned. (If you're stenciling with acrylic paints, and need to mix or thin paints from a jar or tube, use an aluminum palette and a palette knife.) Paints specially developed for stenciling and other types of decorative painting are usually prediluted to the correct consistency and are available in a wide range of colors.

All of these paints are water-soluble; clean spills with soapy water before the paint dries.

Cutting equipment

The type of cutting tool you use depends largely on personal preference. Be sure, though, to use a cutting tool with removable blades, and to always use a sharp blade. A crisply cut stencil creates a sharper image.

Most stencil artists prefer to cut stencils on a piece of glass. Use glass that is at least ¼ inch thick. Protect your fingers by covering the edges of the glass with tape.

Stenciling equipment

Other basic equipment you'll need to cut stencils include tracing paper (to transfer patterns), good-quality masking tape, a pencil and ruler, and a fine-point permanent marker for transferring the patterns to the acetate and for labeling each stencil.

Painting equipment

Unless you're stenciling onto an object that's already painted, you'll need basic painting supplies to apply the base coat. Gather a selection of paintbrushes, sandpaper, steel wool, and a tack cloth.

Design Sources

Because of the two-dimensional nature of stenciling, most designs are simply patterns or outline drawings. Sources of suitable patterns are abundant; investigate the designs on fabric, wallpaper, greeting cards, and gift wrap, and the many stencil-pattern books that feature traditional stencil motifs.

Look for patterns that are simple, can be broken down into basic shapes, and can be interpreted in just a few colors. To change the size of a pattern, use a photocopier with reduction or enlargement capabilities.

1 Trace the cutting lines with solid lines, the registration marks with dashed lines.

2 Use a sharp knife to cut away portions of acetate that correspond to stenciled areas.

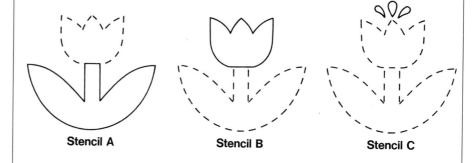

Stencil A   Stencil B   Stencil C

Cutting Stencils

After the pattern is established, the first step is to cut the stencil or series of stencils necessary to reproduce the design.

Cut a piece of acetate for each stencil; be sure to start with a piece large enough to encompass the pattern and a several-inch margin. A large margin around the cut stencil will make the stencil sturdier, as well as protect the stenciled surface from drips and spatters.

Begin by drawing the outline onto tracing paper with a fine-point permanent marker. Then secure the tracing to a flat work surface. Position and tape a piece of acetate over the tracing and, with a marker, trace the outline of just the area to be stenciled. Trace the area to be cut away with a *solid* line. See photo 1, *above*.

If the design requires a second or third stencil, transfer registration markings to the stencil.

Registration markings are the outlines of adjacent stenciled shapes. They serve as guides when you position successive stencils. Draw registration margins with a *broken* line. If a design is comprised of only one stencil, registration markings are not necessary. Label each stencil. See illustration, *above*.

When all tracing is completed, remove the acetate from the outline tracing. Transfer the acetate to a glass cutting surface. Using the cutting tool you find most comfortable, cut the acetate along solid lines. See photo 2, *above*. (For best results, practice first on an acetate scrap.) Repeat for each stencil.

When cutting stencils, always use a sharp blade. Make cuts through the stencil material in single strokes; avoid going over cuts. Hold the knife perpendicular to the cutting surface (or in the most comfortable position); cut with firm, even pressure.

STENCILING PRIMER

Getting Ready To Stencil

A stenciled design will only be as good as the surface on which it's painted. Make sure that any surface you plan to stencil onto is smooth, thoroughly dry, and clean.

Using a ruler and chalk pencil, lightly mark any necessary centerlines or baselines before beginning to stencil. If stencils are to be spaced evenly (around the perimeter of a circle, for example), mark the surface with a chalk pencil as needed. Chalk lines are easy to remove with a damp rag after the stenciled area is dry.

Assemble your materials and equipment in a work area with adequate light. Cover the tabletop with clean paper or a drop cloth. Avoid using newspaper to cover a work surface; ink can rub off onto your work. Although stenciling—when done correctly—uses a minimum of paint, there's always the chance of drips and spatters. Keep a supply of clean rags handy so that you can wipe up spilled paint at once.

Most paints specially formulated for stenciling are ready to use from the jar or bottle. Acrylic paints that come in tubes may have to be thinned to the consistency of heavy cream before stenciling. Use a palette knife to mix a tiny amount of water into the paint, or to blend colors until the desired shade is obtained. Mixing paint requires a bit of practice; experiment before beginning to stencil. Keep in mind that matching fresh paint to paint that has dried is difficult, so prepare enough paint to complete all the stenciling for a particular project.

Stenciling Designs

Before using a newly cut stencil on the actual project surface, practice with it. Do your dry runs on a scrap of illustration board or heavy paper. These tests will enable you to see if the registration marks are correctly positioned, to check if each stencil area is gracefully and properly shaped, and to confirm that all the elements align correctly. Check the color combination, too; if the colors you've mixed don't look right to you, make necessary adjustments.

To begin stenciling, position the first stencil (stencil A) on the object; secure in place with masking tape. Note any registration markings on the stencil when taping it in place, and, if necessary, align it with a baseline or centerline. See photo 1, *below.*

Use a *dry* stencil brush with a bristle size proportional to the area to be stenciled. Dip just the ends of the bristles into the paint. Tap the brush several times onto a newspaper or layers of paper towel to remove the excess paint. (*Note:* Stenciling is a dry-brush painting technique. Beginners often put too much paint on the brush, which causes the paint to seep under the edges of the stencil and create blotches.) Practice loading the brush until you get a good sense for just how much paint is needed to cover an area evenly. See photo 2, *below.*

Tapping the brush in an up-and-down motion, begin applying paint to the stencil area. Work quickly and with a light touch. When using fast-drying acrylic paints, work over an area several times until it is sufficiently covered. Building thin layers of paint is preferable to attempting to cover a surface with just one application of paint.

Small stenciled areas may require just two or three taps to cover the area sufficiently. On large stencil areas, work around the outline of the shape first. Be sure to hold the brush perpendicular to the painted surface when working along the edges of the stencil; holding the brush at an angle may push the paint under the stencil and distort the shape. See photo 3, *below.*

Continue to cover the stencil area completely. See photo 4, *opposite.* Strive for consistent coverage. Some stencil artists prefer to completely cover the area with a solid coat of paint; others

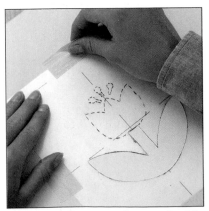

1 Prepare the surface and add any guidelines with a chalk pencil. Align the first stencil and secure with masking tape.

2 Dip just the ends of the brush into the paint. Using an up-and-down motion, tap excess paint onto a paper towel.

3 Make small quick strokes to cover a stencil area. Work around the outside edges of the shape first.

prefer to let just a hint of the background color show through.

When all the area is covered with paint, carefully remove the stencil. Let the paint dry *thoroughly.* Position the next stencil and continue with the second color. See photo 5, *below.*

Combining Stencils

Although lovely stenciling effects are possible with just one color of paint, many stencil artists choose to combine colors in a single design.

With some designs, it is possible to cut out all the stencil areas from just a single piece of acetate. By masking areas, stenciling, and repositioning the masks, you can apply different colors to separate areas of the

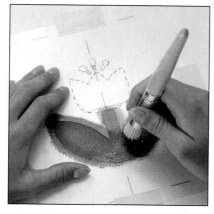

4 Fill in the center of stencil area. Apply paint in layers; avoid using too much paint.

stencil. This works best when only a few colors are used and the different-colored areas are separated.

Most stencil artists prefer to cut separate stencils for each color of paint used. This eliminates the tedious steps of masking and remasking areas, and is much less confusing. The instructions for most of the projects in this book that require the application of more than one color are written according to this latter procedure.

When stenciling complicated or repeated designs, the secret to a successful job is to work out all the details before applying the first dabs of paint. Take measurements first—of both the stencil itself and the area to be stenciled—and work out the mathematics of centering or otherwise positioning the motifs.

5 Remove the stencil and let the paint dry. Align the next stencil with registration marks.

In most cases, positioning the first stencil is the most important step. Once its position is established, the remaining stencils can be placed in relation to it.

The progression of stencils in photo 6, *below,* shows the steps involved in stenciling a design that uses three stencils—and three colors of paint.

Finishing

After the stenciling is completed, the painted design should be protected with polyurethane varnish or a similar clear finish. Although acrylic and latex paints are quite durable, they form only a thin skin on a wooden surface and are easily scratched.

Before finishing, remove any pencil or chalk positioning marks. A kneaded eraser will remove pencil marks; a damp rag will remove chalk marks. Acrylic paints dry quickly and stray drips are difficult to remove; conceal drips of acrylic paint with a touch-up coat of the latex paint used for the base coat. Touch up stenciled areas, if necessary, with quick dabs of stencil paint using a small stencil brush or a cotton swab.

If you'd like to antique the object, do so before applying the finish coat. Use commercially prepared antique finish, or dilute some raw or burnt umber acrylic paint. Brush or wipe on the diluted paint; quickly wipe away the excess paint with a clean rag. (To create a framed effect, remove most of the paint from the center and leave more of it around the edges.) Let the antiquing dry.

Two coats of polyurethane varnish, or a similar clear finish, are usually sufficient to protect a painted surface. Follow manufacturer's directions.

It's a good idea to let any painted surface cure for a few days before applying coats of varnish. And if you have adequate time, wait for a day when humidity is low; this facilitates drying.

6 This sample shows how three stencils combine to create a design. The stem and leaves, *left,* were created with the first stencil. The flower, *center,* was added using the second stencil. Accents, *right,* were painted with the third stencil.

STENCILING PRIMER

Stenciling Onto Fabric

Largely due to improvements in available paints, stenciling onto fabric is now becoming possible. Try stenciling some of the designs in this book onto fabric; many patterns are appropriate for table and window coverings, kitchen and bathroom accessories, and wearables.

Almost any fabric can be stenciled; beginners might have the best results with sturdily woven fabric. Washable fabric should be washed and pressed before stenciling. This not only pre-shrinks the fabric, but it also removes sizing that could interfere with the paint's ability to adhere to the fabric.

To stencil onto washable fabrics, use acrylic paints or textile paints (available at art-supply stores). For fabrics that can't be washed, use textile paints.

Because every fabric will have a different thread texture and a distinctive weave, and will absorb liquids to varying degrees, the consistency of the paint you use is critical. Sheer fabrics require thicker paint; dense fabrics require thinner paint.

If possible, use a scrap of the fabric to test the paint and colors before beginning to stencil. (If a scrap of the fabric isn't available, search for a scrap with similar fiber content and texture.) Keep in mind that the color of the fabric will affect the color of the painted area.

Once the consistency of the paint is satisfactory, proceed with the steps as for stenciling onto painted surfaces. To keep the paint from puddling, you should stencil onto fabric a bit more forcefully than you do onto painted surfaces.

Stenciling Onto Walls

Much of the stenciling that remains from the 18th and 19th centuries is work that was done on walls and ceilings. Stenciled patterns satisfied colonial and Victorian tastes for elaborate ornamentation, and were inexpensive substitutes for printed wallpaper.

Today, stenciling onto walls is again popular, with patterns ranging from 18th-century pineapple motifs to scrolled Victorian friezes to playful contemporary designs.

Although none of the patterns in this book is shown on a wall, many of them are appropriate for this use. Explore the possibility of enlarging some of the designs so that they are more visible, and are easier to stencil onto a wall; or combine some of the motifs to create a border.

Because most wall stenciling is comprised of repeat patterns, planning is important. For simple border designs near the ceiling or above a chair rail, begin the pattern in an inconspicuous corner (as you would a wallpaper border). Then wrap the design along the walls, compensating for the architectural contours of the room.

More complicated patterns might involve careful spacing of motifs. Swags or scrolls, for example, often must align with vertical stenciled motifs. Before beginning, take careful measurements of the surface to be covered. Make scale drawings on graph paper to position all of the elements. To position vertical guidelines on walls, use a carpenter's plumb line.

New Ideas For Stenciling

Because stenciling is such a straightforward painting technique, it's a natural for innovation and experimentation. Following are some suggestions for new approaches to stenciling that you might like to try.

Wax-resist dyeing

This technique will only work on an unfinished wood background. Position and tape a stencil to the wood. Using a stencil brush and neutral shoe polish (in paste form), stencil the area with shoe polish. Remove the stencil and let the surface dry until no wax comes off when you touch the polish.

Mix two parts of liquid dye to one part of cold water. Wipe the dye onto the exposed wood surfaces with a paper towel; dye will not penetrate the polish. Let the dye dry.

To remove the polish, work in a well-ventilated area. Pour a thin coat of turpentine over the wood; let it soak into the polish for a few minutes. Scrub the polished areas with a vegetable brush until the polish is removed. Wipe away the turpentine until the wood feels dry. Finish the surface with polyurethane.

Spatter painting

Usually seen as a method to cover an entire painted surface, spatter painting also works in stenciled areas. Use it exclusively on a given project, or to add accents to conventionally stenciled work.

Dilute stencil paint until it is watery. Dip a stiff-bristled brush (a toothbrush, for example) into the paint. Shake the brush once or twice over paper towels to remove most of the drips. Then, with your thumb, flick the bristles over the stencil.

Spray stenciling

Some beautiful effects are possible with spray paints. Reserve this technique, however, for stenciled areas that don't have a lot of detail. Hold the can of paint (or artist's airbrush equipment) perpendicular to the stencil. Spray quickly and evenly.

Metallic effects

Applying touches of metallic powders to stenciled areas is a centuries-old technique. Areas entirely stenciled with metallics are likely to be overwhelming; use metallics to accent painted work on dark backgrounds.

Metallic powders—available in gold, silver, copper, as well as colors—are sold at art-supply stores. Apply powders with a velvet bob made from a square of velvet wrapped around a wad of polyester fiberfill and tied securely. (Make a bob for each color.)

Work on a day when the air is clear and dry. First, cover the stenciled area with clear varnish; use a stencil brush and very little varnish. Leave the stencil in place and wait until the varnish is tacky. Dip the bob into the powder and tap off the excess. Using a light, circular motion, rub the bob over the varnish. Remove the stencil.

Immediately clean stray powder from the background areas. Let the varnish dry thoroughly. Wash the stenciled area with mild soap and water before applying the final coat of varnish.

Tips from the Pros

Experienced stencil artists often develop their own methods for stenciling, altering some of the basic steps to suit their needs. Following are some tips and shortcuts that you can incorporate into your own stenciling repertoire.

Handling stencils
● To repair a torn stencil, affix transparent tape over the tear, on both the front and the back of the stencil. Trim excess tape from stencil cutouts with a knife; don't fold the tape under the edge of the stencil.
● Although stencils will last for many years, a buildup of stencil paint on the edges of a cutout may alter the shape of the design slightly or prevent the stencil from lying flat. To clean a stencil, moisten a paper towel with a small amount of isopropyl alcohol. Lay the stencil out on a flat surface and rub the stencil with the towel; work from the outside toward the cut areas.
● Test the stickiness of your tape before affixing a stencil to a painted surface. Some brands and types of tape are so sticky

Sources for Stenciling Materials

Crafts-supply stores in your area are likely to carry everything you'll need for stenciling, including brushes, stencil paints, and other painting equipment. Write to the manufacturers and distributors listed below for information concerning their stenciling supplies and unfinished wooden items.

Stencil paints and equipment

Adele Bishop, Inc.
 P.O. Box 3349
 Kinston, NC 28501

Illinois Bronze Paint Co.
 Craft Finishes Division
 300 E. Main St.
 Lake Zurich, IL 60047

Plaid Enterprises, Inc.
 P.O. Box 7600
 Norcross, GA 30091

Stencil World
 8 W. 19th Street
 New York, NY 10011

Unfinished wooden accessories

Basketville, Inc.
 R.R. 1
 Putney, VT 05346

Demis Products, Inc.
 2000 Jabco Dr.
 P.O. Box 348
 Lithonia, GA 30058

Sudberry House
 P.O. Box 895
 Old Lyme, CT 06371

Walnut Hollow Farm
 R.R. 2
 Dodgeville, WI 53533

Weston Bowl Mill
 Main St.
 Weston, VT 05161

Yield House
 33 Elm St.
 Merrimack, NH 03054

that they will destroy the base coat when you remove them. To reduce a tape's stickiness, stick the tape to a fabric scrap several times before using it.

Preparing surfaces
● Waxed or high-gloss surfaces are not suitable for stenciling with acrylic paints. To stencil over a high-gloss surface, roughen the surface first with a coating of matte-finish acrylic spray.
● Sometimes a background color is not suitable for all of the colors that are to be stenciled onto it. If you fear this might be the case with your background color, stencil an undercoat of the desired shape before adding the color. For example, if you're stenciling a pale pink flower onto a dark green background, first stencil the flower shape with white or a slightly lighter

green color. Let this shape dry and then stencil the pink flower on top.

Applying paint
● Some expert stencil artists prefer to apply paint to stencil areas with sponges instead of more costly brushes. To do this, cut a piece of sponge proportional to the stencil area. Dip one end into the stencil paint, tap off the excess paint onto paper towels, and proceed as for stenciling with a brush.
● When you're stenciling large areas or many repeats, paint may build up in the bristles and make your brush stiff. Dip the bristles into mineral spirits and wipe them with a scrubbing motion onto paper towels. Shake the excess liquid from the brush and let it dry thoroughly before continuing.

ACKNOWLEDGMENTS

Our special thanks to the following designers who contributed projects to this book. When more than one project appears on a page, the acknowledgment specifically cites the project with the page number. A page number alone indicates one designer or source has contributed all of the project material listed for that page.

Pam Dyer—38–43

Alice Fjelstul—58–59

Sally Paul—4–5; 24–27

Rosa Snyder—6–11; 28–29; 52–57; 60–61

We also are pleased to acknowledge the following photographers, whose talents and technical skills contributed much to this book.

Hopkins Associates—4–11; 24–29; 38–43; 52–61

Perry Struse—74–77

For their creative skills, courtesy, and cooperation, we extend a special thanks to:

Marianne Fons

Peggy Leonardo

Margaret Sindelar

Don Wipperman

For their cooperation and courtesy, we extend a special thanks to the following sources:

Laura Ashley (for tea set pictured on pages 6–7)
714 Madison Ave.
New York, NY 10021

Benartex, Inc. (for "My Tulip Garden" fabrics pictured on pages 38–39 and 41)
1412 Broadway
New York, NY 10018

Plaid Enterprises, Inc. (for Stencil Decor paints)
P.O. Box 7600
Norcross, GA 30091

Have BETTER HOMES AND GARDENS® magazine delivered to your door. For information, write to:
MR. ROBERT AUSTIN
P.O. BOX 4536
DES MOINES, IA 50336